Date: 9/30/16

241.68 DOL
Dollar, Creflo A.
You're supposed to be
wealthy : how to make

YOU'RE
SUPPOSED
TO BE
WEALTHY

Books by Dr. Creflo Dollar

In the Presence of God

Live Without Fear

Not Guilty

Love, Live, and Enjoy Life

Breaking Out of Trouble

Walking in the Confidence of God in Troubled Times

Claim Your Victory Today

Winning in Troubled Times

The Holy Spirit, Your Financial Advisor

Real Manhood

YOU'RE SUPPOSED TO BE WEALTHY

How to Make Money,
Live Comfortably, and
Build an Inheritance
for Future Generations

DR. CREFLO DOLLAR

Faith
Words

NEW YORK   BOSTON   NASHVILLE

Unless otherwise indicated, all Scripture quotations are from the King James
Version of the Holy Bible.

Scripture quotations taken from the New American Standard Bible®,
Copyright © 1960, 1962, 1963, 1968, 1971, 1972, 1973, 1975, 1977, 1995 by
The Lockman Foundation. Used by permission. (www.Lockman.org)

FaithWords
Hachette Book Group
237 Park Avenue
New York, NY 10017

faithwords.com

Printed in the United States of America

RRD-C

First Edition: September 2014
10 9 8 7 6 5 4 3 2 1

FaithWords is a division of Hachette Book Group, Inc.
The FaithWords name and logo are trademarks of Hachette Book Group, Inc.

The Hachette Speakers Bureau provides a wide range of authors for speaking
events. To find out more, go to www.hachettespeakersbureau.com or call
(866) 376-6591.

The publisher is not responsible for websites (or their content) that are not
owned by the publisher.

Library of Congress Cataloging-in-Publication Data

Dollar, Creflo A.
  You're supposed to be wealthy : how to make money, live comfortably, and
build an inheritance for future generations / Dr. Creflo Dollar. — First Edition.
    pages cm
    ISBN 978-1-4555-7736-1 (hardcover) — ISBN 978-1-4555-3011-3 (large print
hardcover) — ISBN 978-1-4555-7733-0 (ebook) — ISBN 978-1-4789-5550-4
(audiobook) — ISBN 978-1-4789-5551-1 (audio download)   1. Wealth—
Religious aspects—Christianity.   2. Finance, Personal—Religious
aspects—Christianity.   I. Title.
  BR115.W4D65 2014
  241'.68—dc23
                        2014010762

CONTENTS

INTRODUCTION

As the return of the Lord Jesus Christ draws near, it is imperative that Christians be able to clearly discern the Holy Spirit's voice in every area of their lives. One of the areas where God desires to bring clarity, understanding, and purpose is in the area of finances. Believers have so many misconceptions about money that many of them have no idea what God's will is regarding the finances of His people. As a result, they remain in financial lack and poverty without knowing God's plan for their lives. By tapping into the wisdom of God, however, Christians can learn what it truly means to be prosperous. By following His leading, individuals can make sound financial decisions and wise investments that will enable them not only to make money and live comfortably, but also to build an inheritance for future generations.

When it comes to biblical prosperity, there are some important things to keep in mind. First, it is God's will for Christians to prosper financially. We know that prosperity isn't limited to money, but money is one part of the prosperity pie. We've been conditioned to believe that a person who has a lot of money is prosperous, and certainly happy. We know this isn't the case because many people have plenty of money but are miserable. Having finances without peace of mind, health, and flourishing, loving relationships gives a picture of incomplete prosperity. We want to make sure that we are operating in abundance not only where finances are concerned but also in every other area of our lives.

With that being said, it is important to understand the difference between being rich and being *wealthy*. When a person is rich, it simply means he or she has a lot of money—at the moment. To be wealthy is something different. Wealth starts with a mind-set. Even though someone may have a lot of money in his or her bank account, that person can still have a poverty mind-set rather than a wealthy mind-set. A poverty mind-set will always lead to the dwindling of finances rather than increase, meaning that the person with money will eventually end up at square one, with little to nothing. Similarly, when a person has a wealthy mind-set, it is only a matter of time before his or her bank account goes from $10 to $10 million. This is because wealth begins with the way we think, regardless of what we have in our possession.

Wealth starts with a mind-set.

People with a wealthy mind-set think and act differently from those who are poverty-minded. Wealth means you not only have money, but you are also establishing an inheritance for future generations. This inheritance can include anything from material assets, such as antiques and collectibles that have been passed down from generation to generation, to stock, real estate, and annuities that can be liquidated or kept in an interest-bearing account such as an IRA, CD, or money market account. When you are operating in generational wealth, you are thinking and investing in your future and in the futures of your descendants.

Christians are called to be wealthy, just as our heavenly Father is wealthy; however, achieving the will of God concerning our finances is going to require tangible and intangible strategies to get us to that ultimate destination of wealth *and* riches. Obedience to the voice of the Holy Spirit and understanding the three keys to proper stewardship, combined with practical knowledge of the various types of investment methods and strategies, will enable Believers to experience financial prosperity and success.

*Christians are called to be wealthy, just
as our heavenly Father is wealthy.*

One of the biggest hindrances to achieving true and lasting wealth is a person's mind-set, which is why renewing the mind is so vital to this process. Most of us have been raised with ideas about money that did not line up with the Word, thus giving us an incomplete or inaccurate picture of prosperity. Some of us were raised with the idea that having a lot of money is ungodly, or that wealth will never be a reality. Others are dealing with poverty mind-sets that have been passed down from generation to generation.

The truth is, if you are going to walk in the level of prosperity that is available to you through God's Word, which includes wealth, you're going to have to get serious about renewing your mind. Failing to do so means allowing your old ideas and old ways of thinking to continue to block what God is trying to get you to realize concerning your financial prosperity. When your mind has not been renewed, you tend to function with a "lack" mentality, while God is trying to show you something better.

It is also important that we understand the objective of wealth. If we don't understand the purpose for something, the abuse of it is inevitable. Wealth is designed to enable us to establish God's covenant in the earth through our ability to bless people until *all* families of the earth are blessed. Being wealthy isn't just about you; it is always about other people. God wants us to enjoy our wealth and enjoy life, but the primary focus of acquiring wealth is so that we can advance the kingdom of God and establish the blessing in the earth in tangible form. When we create a generational legacy of wealth, we perpetuate the blessing through our children and grandchildren and carry out the generational mandate God has given us to establish His covenant in this earth.

Transformation starts with the mind, and if you are going to move from where you are presently to the level of wealth God has designed for you, you will have to allow your life to be transformed by saturating yourself in the meditation of God's Word on finances, specifically as it relates to wealth and material increase. This also means making a quality decision to reject ways of thinking that you may have grown up with, or the mind-sets of your friends and family. God never created us to think and behave as if we were not worthy of the best that life has to offer. He wants us to think and behave like the King's kids we are! We are surrounded by deception on every side about the issue of finances and the role it plays in the Christian's life. But I'm here to tell you not to receive it. To be successful in the financial arena, you have to get in the presence of the Word, read, study, and meditate on it, and act on the direction of the Holy Spirit.

Moving toward true financial and material wealth is also going to take some decisions of quality where our financial habits and practices are concerned. It is going to take moving from a hyper-consumption mentality to a more modest financial approach when it comes to consuming goods and services. Someone who is not concerned with building a lasting wealth legacy will live for the enjoyment of today rather than the future. All too often we allow our lusts for the material trappings of this world to drive our spending habits, which usually leaves us in debt and shortage. We may have a beautiful wardrobe or a new car, but no savings! We buy things that *depreciate* in value rather than investing in things that will *appreciate* over time. Then we wonder why we seem to remain financially unstable.

This book will absolutely transform your life by giving you not only the spiritual direction you need to understand wealth and finances but also the practical tools you need to begin creating wealth now. Consider the information found here and commit to renewing your mind and changing your financial behavior. Building wealth is not difficult, but it does take discipline and commitment to your future. You can start creating a legacy of wealth for your family and those who will come after you when you are gone. The power is in your hands, and the choice is yours, so start today. You're supposed to be rich!

The power is in your hands, and the choice
is yours, so start today.

YOU'RE
SUPPOSED
TO BE
WEALTHY

UNDERSTANDING GOD'S WILL FOR YOUR LIFE CONCERNING YOUR FINANCES

But my God shall supply all your need according
to his riches in glory by Christ Jesus.

—PHILIPPIANS 4:19

Wisdom and knowledge is granted unto thee;
and I will give thee riches, and wealth, and
honour, such as none of the kings have had
that have been before thee, neither shall
there any after thee have the like.

—2 CHRONICLES 1:12

When it comes to money, the body of Christ is not where it should be. It is not God's will for the ungodly rich of this world to be the biggest givers and the most notable financiers of charitable outreaches. God desires that His people walk in a level of financial prosperity that surpasses the world's. But we must renew our minds to the truth about wealth according to God's Word. The enemy knows that if he can keep resources out of our hands, we cannot be as effective in the kingdom. It takes money to do all that God has called us to do, which is why we must move out of the arena of "just enough" and grow to the arena of "more than enough." When we have more than enough, we can truly begin to establish God's covenant in the earth by being a blessing to others until all families of the earth are blessed beyond measure.

There is a difference between wealth and riches, and while God does want us to enjoy both (Ecclesiastes 5:18–19, 6:1–2), we should understand the distinction between the two. Riches can be described as abundance that can be converted into material things. Cars, clothes, jewelry, and other high-end items that cost a lot of money fall into the category of "riches." Riches typically depreciate over time and eventually expire. Riches are highly visible, and people have a tendency to show off their material possessions if they are not careful. These types of items are also looked at in terms of price and are driven by advertising. An immature person will tend to focus on acquiring riches, rather than on taking further steps to acquire wealth.

When we talk about wealth, it takes the conversation up a notch because wealth is measured in terms of time. In other words, the amount of time you can live off your current resources without actually having to work for a living is a good gauge for determining how "wealthy" you are. Wealth not only deals with having money in your bank account but also the ability to establish an inheritance for future generations. Included in this inheritance are other things besides liquid cash, such as antiques, collectibles, stocks, real estate, and other assets that appreciate in value as time goes on.

Another characteristic of wealth that makes it different from riches is the fact that wealth appreciates and endures over time rather than depreciates. For example, the acquisition of real estate is a wealth-building strategy because homes build equity, which is a benefit to the owner in the long run. This is an example of *appreciation*, or an increase in value over time. Wealth is not often visible but is hidden, unlike riches, which can be seen by others. Often, a person's wealth is tied up in unseen investments that aren't outwardly evident. Wealth is all about making wise decisions with your resources today, so that you can build a better tomorrow for yourself and your family. It has everything to do with planning and accounting. Generational wealth and riches should be the financial goal and objective of every Believer.

Wealth is not often visible but is hidden, unlike riches, which can be seen by others.

It is not wrong to have wealth and riches. In fact, the Word has so much to say about finances that it is a topic we cannot ignore. If we can find something in the Word, we can take it to the bank because it is a promise. Our part is to release our faith in God's grace to bring the promise of wealth to pass in our lives.

Psalm 112:1–3 paints a picture of abundance (both spiritually and financially) that we would do well to study. It says, "Praise ye the LORD. Blessed is the man that feareth the LORD, that delighteth greatly in his commandments. His seed shall be mighty upon the earth: the generation of the upright shall be blessed. Wealth and riches shall be in his house: and his righteousness endureth for ever."

This passage deals with both the intangible and tangible aspects of prosperity. Before the writer even gets to the manifestation of wealth and riches, he mentions the relationship the truly wealthy person has with the Lord. He says that the person who fears or reverences God is empowered to prosper, or is *blessed*. This person who fears the Lord does so by holding the Word in the highest regard and delighting in God's instructions. Flowing from this person's thriving relationship with God is the manifestation of wealth and riches. In addition, his righteous character is a legacy that will never be forgotten.

When our relationship with God is intact and we are honoring His Word, how do we get from a place of lack and insufficiency to a place of abundance? Moreover, how do we go even further to a place of operating on a level of wealth and riches that can be translated into a tangible generational blessing? Understanding the levels of prosperity is critical to reaching this point, as well as understanding that acquiring wealth is more about effectively managing and handling the money you have through specific strategies and financial principles than anything else.

The Blessing of Wealth

God wants us to be rich! He also wants us to leave a legacy of wealth to our grandchildren and beyond. Yet becoming wealthy is not going to happen simply because it is in the Word or we know about it. We must engage certain principles and do certain practical things in order to see these financial blessings become a reality. The first step is to renew our minds with the truth of God's Word on this issue. We must understand that poverty, lack, and insufficiency are *not* the will of God. Abundance, prosperity, and wealth are part of God's plan for our lives. Everyone is not going to be wealthy, but everyone *can* be. We have to go back to God's original plan for mankind to understand this.

Becoming wealthy is not going to happen simply because it is in the Word or we know about it.

When God created man, He had three primary intentions that are outlined in Scripture. Genesis 1:26–29 tells us what those intentions are. It says:

> And God said, Let us make man in our image, after our likeness: and let them have dominion over the fish of the sea, and over the fowl of the air, and over the cattle, and over all the earth, and over every creeping thing that creepeth upon the earth. So God created man in his own image, in the image of God created he him; male and female created he them. And God blessed them, and God said unto them, Be fruitful, and multiply, and replenish the earth, and subdue it:

and have dominion over the fish of the sea, and over the fowl of the air, and over every living thing that moveth upon the earth. And God said, Behold, I have given you every herb bearing seed, which is upon the face of all the earth.

The first thing God did after creating mankind was bless them. The blessing is an empowerment for success. We have been spiritually equipped with a supernatural empowerment that enables us to get results in every area of our lives, including the financial arena. The second thing God did was give us dominion, or authority over the earth, which includes its resources. We have dominion over anything that can be produced in the earth, including money. There is no reason for us to be living in poverty and lack when we have authority over the material realm. Finally, God gave us seed, which is the catalyst for increase. These three components form the basis for our wealth-building efforts.

The first thing God did after creating mankind was bless them.

It is unfortunate to see people who don't even believe in Jesus Christ achieving results in the financial realm that those who are born-again seem not to have been able to tap into. Many wealthy people in the world are able to do more for those in need than those in the body of Christ can do, which is a shame. Wealth is a part of the blessing God bestowed on mankind; poverty is part of the curse. The body of Christ is supposed to be God's hands in the earth, distributing His resources to those who are in need and creating a vehicle for establishing the covenant of blessing in the earth.

When we look at how Adam and Eve lived in the Garden of Eden prior to the Fall, we see a true picture of wealth on a holistic level. First, we see that they lived in a lush environment that was abundant with the resources they needed to live. Their food and other needs were provided for, and they never went without. They were surrounded by natural minerals and what would be considered precious resources by today's standards. Everything God created was at their disposal! Not only that, but their lifestyle was saturated with the presence of God, which always results in the abundant life.

From an interpersonal perspective, their relationship was whole and healthy, and they operated in a level of cohesiveness that reflected uninterrupted fellowship with the Father. The condition of their souls was prosperous. They experienced no fear, stress, or negative emotions. They did not have to toil to make ends meet or worry about how they would eat from day to day. They were provided for in every way: spiritually, physically, and emotionally.

This prosperity picture is the will of God for every Believer. It is time for us to get back to the Garden of Eden and reclaim the quality of life that Adam and Eve had the privilege of experiencing. Through our relationship with Jesus Christ, we can, indeed, live this life of fullness.

God's Attitude Toward Us

Where did we get the idea that it is okay to toil, struggle, and live in a perpetual state of insufficiency as Believers? Poverty does not make you more humble; it makes you desperate for resources. Jesus came to restore us to our original state of livelihood. The curse should not be seen in the lives of born-again people, yet many Christians who genuinely love the Lord don't know or understand what they have a right to as it pertains to the financial realm. They don't receive the truth about God's financial will for their lives because they don't believe they can ever go beyond their current financial level (a containment mentality), or they think that wealth will somehow magically happen (which it never does). We should never tolerate anything that is under the curse, but we also have to realize that we have a part to play.

God's attitude toward us is summed up in one word—*blessing*. Sin interrupted the blessing God originally bestowed on man and thrust him into survival mode, forcing him to get by the best he could. However, God restored the blessing in the earth through Noah, Abraham, and ultimately Jesus. Through Jesus, we are Abraham's seed and heirs to the promise of the blessing. We are now living a pre-Fall existence *after* the Fall of man!

> *God's attitude toward us is summed up in one word—*blessing.

God is interested in the financial component of your life and He wants you to be wealthy. In Christ, any man can become an heir of the blessing, which includes material wealth and riches. Proverbs 10:22 says, "The blessing of the Lord, it maketh rich, and he addeth no sorrow with it." When God blesses you with wealth and financial prosperity, no curse is attached to it, unlike those who acquire wealth outside of God's blessing, or through ungodly means. Peace in your soul is the added benefit of doing things God's way.

The Levels of Financial Prosperity

Let's examine the different financial levels people find themselves in and how those levels form a foundation that can ultimately lead to wealth. The first is the provision level. It can also be looked at as the "needs" phase. It is at this stage that your basic needs are being met. This is also the stage that is usually the most painful and emotionally taxing because what looks like perpetual lack is very stressful. We have all been there at some point in our lives. The good news is that God promises to meet our needs according to His riches in glory, through Christ Jesus (Philippians 4:19). Many times people get needs confused with *wants*. A need is something that you *must* have in life such as food, clothing, water, a roof over your head, medical care, electricity, transportation, etc. We need to pay our bills every month because that ensures that we keep up the basics as they relate to our living situations.

The good news is that God promises to meet our needs according to His riches in glory, through Christ Jesus (Philippians 4:19).

It is often in the needs phase that it may seem we are living from miracle to miracle. We may not know where the money is coming from to pay our bills or buy food because there is no reserve or financial cushion in the bank account. The challenge in this stage is to continue tithing, giving, and sharing resources with others in the midst of what looks like a shortage of finances. Obedience to God's instructions, even though things are tight, is critical to receiving more. If we master kingdom principles during the needs phase, it opens the door to expansion and increase.

This phase is where the Believer *really* learns how to trust God on a moment-by-moment basis. It is also where we will build a monument of reminders of how God will always provide for us when we trust in Him and release our faith in His Word.

The next financial level is the sufficiency level. This is the stage most people reach and remain in for the majority of their lives. *Sufficiency* can be defined as "having as much as is desired or enough" (*Webster's Dictionary*). When you are in the sufficiency stage, you are no longer living miracle to miracle and your needs are definitely met. You are not barely getting by anymore, and you don't require any outside aid or support from anyone. You are able to give and be obedient to God's kingdom instructions and even help create sufficiency in someone else's life from time to time. One of the tendencies, however, is to become fearful of returning to the provision stage, so you may be tempted to withhold in the area of giving.

Third is the abundance level. At this stage your needs are met, you have enough, and you have extra, which translates to your having more options in life. You are able to give liberally and to fulfill all the kingdom requirements God asks of you, such as tithing, first fruits, offerings, etc. You are able to see some of your desires fulfilled and other people can also see that God is prospering you. While this is quite a step of financial growth from the needs phase, it is also the phase at which many people hit a plateau or even regress because they start getting into hyperconsumption. Instead of being wise with their finances, they may allow lust and a lack of discipline to consume the resources they have.

Reaching the abundance stage requires a balance of being generous toward the kingdom of God, being generous toward others, and enjoying some of the abundance yourself. It is a crossroads phase that will determine whether you ever get to the place of being wealthy. Being a good steward over the "extra" that comes into your hands is the test you must pass if you are going to get to the next stage, which is wealth and riches.

As I stated earlier in this chapter, wealth is essentially defined in terms of time. In other words, how long would you be able to sustain your current lifestyle if you were not working? The longer you can sustain, the wealthier you are. When you are operating in true wealth, you also have resources that can be applied to future generations, including your children's children. At this stage you are beyond abundance and are able to position yourself to move into the aspect of financial legacy, which will sustain others even after you are gone.

The longer you can sustain, the wealthier you are.

Motives Are Everything

The question of whether or not God wants us to be wealthy is something that is not up for debate. The answer is an emphatic *yes*! We must constantly judge our lives, however, to make sure our motives are pure. God will not allow us to walk in the highest level of financial prosperity if:

- We have the wrong priorities.
- We put our trust in money.

- Our finances are directed toward only ourselves.

- We take advantage of others to become wealthy and gain riches.

- We allow money to hinder us from following God or obeying Him.

- We allow money to give us a sense of superiority over others.

- We fail to give generously.

- We find our life's meaning and sense of self-worth in our material possessions.

- We think we no longer need God.

- We refuse to deal with areas of sin in our lives.

- We allow money to cost us our peace and put it before our relationships with others.

- We allow ourselves to be completely focused on acquiring more material possessions.

- We allow money to mean more to us than it should.

First Timothy 6:10 says, "The love of money is the root of all evil." This simply means that it is our wrong relationship with money and material resources that is the problem, not the money itself. The love of money is essentially a character issue that must be resolved because money will only amplify whatever character issues a person has. This is another reason why many Christians have yet to walk in true biblical wealth. It is because their character is not developed to the point of being able to handle it. God wants us to be rich if we can maintain our righteousness before God. That is the test we all must pass, which is why He allows us to progress through the different financial levels in preparation for increase and financial promotion.

God wants us to be rich if we can maintain
our righteousness before God.

Learning How to Become Wealthy

You may be in one of the financial stages and wondering how you can get to the place of being wealthy. Or, if you are wealthy, you may be wondering how you can exceed your current wealth level. The key is found in Isaiah 48:17: "Thus saith the LORD, thy Redeemer, the Holy One of Israel; I am the LORD thy God which teacheth thee to profit, which leadeth thee by the way that thou shouldest go." Profit and prosperity come from being *taught* and being led by God. This wisdom comes through information that God has released into the earth in the form of practical knowledge and financial strategies and principles, as well as your ability to hear from the Holy Spirit directly as He leads and guides you in the crucial decisions you must make to ensure your financial future.

Keep in mind that becoming wealthy has an educational aspect; it is not something you just automatically know how to do when money comes into your hands. Mastering your finances is essential to building wealth. Your prosperity has nothing to do with how righteous you are but how much you know and understand basic financial concepts. For example, a basic formula for building wealth is to increase your income or decrease your outflow. When you do this, you create "extra." Anyone who can create "extra" along with increasing his or her skills and discipline can move to the place of wealth and riches. This formula is no respecter of persons but will work for anyone who will get involved.

Your prosperity has nothing to do with how righteous you are but how much you know and understand basic financial concepts.

It is also important to realize that the lessons you learn in the financial stages of provision and sufficiency determine how you will ultimately handle wealth and riches when you get to that point. For example, the primary lesson of the provision stage is that God is your source. In the sufficiency stage, you learn to be content with having just enough. It is during this stage that you learn how to tame your lust and become disciplined in how you spend your money. The abundance phase teaches you that the extra money that comes into your hands has a threefold purpose: to increase the kingdom, to bless others, and to provide for personal enjoyment. If you do not learn and put into practice the lessons of making God your source, practicing financial discipline, and learning how to handle extra money, wealth and riches will destroy you.

There are several ways a Christian can achieve financial increase. They are:

1. Labor/employment or working for someone else.

2. Self-employment.

3. Owning a business or system where you do not spend the majority of your time involved with the daily hands-on aspects of your business. In other words, you hire others to handle those details,

but you reap the financial benefits of the business system you have implemented as it relates to the service you offer.

4. Investments.

5. Inheritance.

6. Wealth transfer.

Since Christians are held to a standard of integrity and honor when it comes to making money, they cannot engage in illegal activities to become wealthy. Therefore, these legitimate avenues are the primary means through which money will come.

As you go through these stages, it is important to remember that no matter what is going on in the economy or the world around us, we are not limited by the world's resources or systems. As children of God operating in the kingdom of God on this earth, we can tap into the resources of heaven by faith in order to receive what is available to us. This means it is indeed possible to become wealthy in the midst of hard times. The story of Isaac is a prime example of this. The Bible says that he sowed during a time of famine and reaped a hundredfold as a result (Genesis 26:12). The famine did not limit Isaac's prosperity. The blessing on his life, coupled with his obedience, positioned him for increase.

It is indeed possible to become wealthy in the midst of hard times.

If your faith in the financial prosperity promises of the Bible is not strong, you are going to need some serious mind renewal to be able to receive what God has for you in this area. This means reading the Bible to find out what God has said and then meditating on biblical prosperity until your thinking begins to change and your capacity to receive expands. Romans 12:1–2 instructs us not to be conformed to the world's way of thinking but to be transformed by the renewing of our minds so that we can prove the good, acceptable, and perfect will of God for our lives. Wealth is God's will for our lives, even though the world wants Christians to believe that the resources of the earth are off-limits to us. There are even those in the church who try to enforce a poverty mind-set in people's lives by preaching against prosperity. But everything God has belongs to His children, through faith in Jesus Christ. That includes wealth and riches.

As I dig deeper into this important topic, I want to remind you again that money is not the root of all evil, but the love of money, or a wrong relationship with money, is the root of all evil. When we try to use money to rectify an inner spiritual issue we may have or to feel better about ourselves, we are out of order. Money cannot solve heart issues; only God can do that. He will allow us to go through certain things in order to build our character to the point where we are able to handle greater levels of financial responsibility. Every character test you pass where money is concerned will position you for promotion and increase. Love must be your motive and your heart must be pure.

It is time for the body of Christ to rise to the level of financial prosperity that God desires for us. The kingdom of God must be advanced in the earth, and it is going to take money to get the job done. No longer can we sit by and allow the world to claim sole ownership of what rightfully belongs to us as Believers. We must learn how to implement and put into practice the financial strategies and wisdom that will take us to the next level. Skill, discipline, and time, combined with the wisdom of God, the grace of God, and the favor of God, will result in supernatural results. We have the advantage; now let's advance into the highest levels of biblical prosperity. We're *supposed* to be rich!

It is time for the body of Christ to rise to the level of financial prosperity that God desires for us.

2

PLAN TO SUCCEED

And God is able to make all grace abound
toward you; that ye, always having all sufficiency
in all things, may abound to every good work:
(As it is written, He hath dispersed abroad;
he hath given to the poor: his righteousness
remaineth for ever. Now he that ministereth
seed to the sower both minister bread for
your food, and multiply your seed sown,
and increase the fruits of your
righteousness;).

—2 CORINTHIANS 9:8–10

I have established that it is God's will for you to prosper financially, but knowledge of this fact is not enough to actually see the manifestation of wealth in your life. Renewing your mind with this truth and putting a plan in place will make the promises of wealth a reality. Having clear-cut financial objectives and then establishing short- and long-term goals is essential to fulfilling your objectives. When you fail to plan, you plan to fail.

When you fail to plan, you plan to fail.

All money has three purposes: to honor God and help others; to life-build, which can be tracked and measured; and to enjoy personally. Your finances will be dispersed among these three categories. The first category describes kingdom-focused financial objectives such as tithing, giving offerings, helping the poor, supporting missions, partnering with ministries that are helping to spread the gospel, etc. It deals with giving to others as the Spirit of God leads you. True satisfaction comes from making this objective your priority. There is nothing like the feeling that comes from knowing you first honored God with your increase, whether it is through tithing, giving, helping the poor, or paying for someone's groceries in the checkout line at the grocery store. Not only that, but kingdom-focused financial objectives form a spiritual foundation that enables you to reap a harvest of financial blessings. The Bible says that when you seek first God's way of doing things, everything else will be added to you (Matthew 6:33).

The second destination of your money is the life-building category. This deals with directing your finances toward taking care of needs in your day-to-day life, as well as saving and investing for your future. It involves things like paying your bills and paying off debt. When your money is going toward present and future life-building, it can be measured and accounted for every step of the way. If you look at where you are now in comparison to where you were six months ago, you should be able to see some positive changes when you are activating life-building financial strategies.

When you are using your money for life-building purposes, you can say, "I have this much in my savings account compared to where I was last year," or "All my bills are paid, and my credit card debts are at a zero balance now." Life-building financial objectives demonstrate traceable progress from one year to the next. Money should be used responsibly to handle the necessities of life as well as to take care of your financial future. Life insurance policies, CDs and other interest-accruing accounts, as well as the purchase of things that appreciate such as homes or other investment properties, are ways you can channel your money into viable life-building ventures that benefit you now and years down the line. These things also lay the groundwork for future wealth.

Finally, there is the enjoyment category. This is an area that many Christians do not believe they should experience. Wrong doctrine and misinterpretation of the Scriptures have led many well-meaning Believers to the conclusion that God does not want them to take pleasure in their finances or that it is a sin to desire material things. The truth is God put many things in this earth for the sole purpose of our enjoyment!

God is not a harsh taskmaster who wants to keep His children from enjoying the fruit of their labor. On the contrary, your heavenly Father wants you to enjoy a portion of the money you have worked hard to acquire. There is nothing wrong with appreciating the fruit of your labor, as long as you don't allow that aspect of wealth to supersede the first two foundational areas. As long as you have taken care of kingdom business and have also done your part in the life-building area, you have every right to partake of some of your "extra." The key is to keep things in balance and never allow enjoyment to overshadow wise decision making where life-building is concerned. Doing so can halt your financial progress and short-circuit your wealth-building objectives.

Once you have an understanding of these three directions in which your money is to flow, you can begin coming up with a plan and strategy for acquiring wealth. One of the mistakes many Christians make concerning finances is that they think the spiritual side of things is the only side they need to be concerned with. While the spiritual aspect is critical, wealth is not just going to drop out of the sky or magically come into your hands because you make confessions and believe it is available to you. You need to do some very practical things in order to set yourself on the path to financial increase.

Establishing Personal Objectives and Setting Goals

Establishing financial objectives is critical to the development of an effective wealth-building plan. Objectives give focus and purpose to your plan and provide a solid foundation for making financial decisions. When coming up with your objectives, think about the things you would like to accomplish in your future.

For example, do you want to be able to assist your grandchildren financially when that time comes? Perhaps you want to save for your child's college education, buy a home, become debt-free, or retire with a nice nest egg. Every goal counts if it is something that is important to you.

You may be reading this information and finding this is the first time you have really sat down even to think about your financial future. Don't be discouraged. It is important to begin somewhere, so why not start now? When trying to come up with your objectives, the following topics may help spark some practical ideas:

1. Wealth Accumulation

Wealth accumulation involves building up your financial reserves. This includes things like building an emergency fund, saving for a child's education, saving for retirement, and providing a source of income from a business venture. A great goal is to have an initial target of three months' savings and an ultimate target of one year of reserves that can be easily liquidated. Remember that wealth is measured in terms of time. In other words, you are wealthy in proportion to how long you can sustain your current lifestyle without having to work. A wealth mind-set looks for ways to build financial security in the future rather than make decisions for the moment at the expense of tomorrow.

A wealth mind-set looks for ways to build financial security in the future rather than make decisions for the moment at the expense of tomorrow.

2. Asset Creation

You may want to own your own home, own a vacation property, invest in real estate/rental property, or collect antiques, jewelry, or artwork. These items can fall under the category of "wealth" because they tend to appreciate with time rather than depreciate. If you are not a homeowner, this should be one of your primary goals. A mortgage is something you can consider a "good debt" because you are investing in an asset that will increase in value over the years. The equity you gain by being a homeowner can be used toward acquiring other properties that can produce more income for you.

3. Protection from Personal Risks

Taking the necessary steps to lay out the financial details of a pre-mature death situation, or estate planning, is an important part of establishing goals and objectives. If you will have surviving family members, you will want the process of making arrangements and handling your assets to go as smoothly as possible. You also may want to ensure financial protection in the event of a long-term disability. In addition, taking out insurance on your personal property is also a wise decision.

Goal setting gives you something to work toward, which is why goals are so critical to your wealth-building strategy. They are specific, tangible, measurable checkpoints that you can start working on now. Try not to be too vague or general when establishing goals. For example, saying, "I want to be rich when I retire" is probably not specific enough to give you a clear picture of how to achieve that goal. But saying, "I want to be able to give ten thousand dollars a year to the kingdom of God after I retire" is a goal that is more clear-cut, focused, and workable, with the right plan in place.

Goal setting gives you something to work toward, which is why goals are so critical to your wealth-building strategy.

Determining your financial goals should encompass both short- and long-term objectives. For example, you may have a short-term goal of paying off a credit card in six months. A long-term goal may be to retire at a specific age with a certain amount of money in your reserve savings. Come up with several short- and long-term goals for your finances and write them down. Once you do that, begin to come up with specific action steps you can take to achieve these goals. You may want to cut back on eating out and put the extra money you spend weekly at restaurants into your savings account. Or you may consider not using credit cards unless you can pay the balance in full at the end of the month. Whatever steps you develop, take action immediately! You will feel that much closer to achieving them when you stop procrastinating.

Another important aspect of setting goals is accountability. Have people around you to whom you are accountable, and don't hesitate to share what you are working on with them. The reinforcement you receive from your accountability team will keep you focused when you feel like giving up. Don't allow what seems like a lengthy journey toward financial freedom and wealth to cause you to cave in and quit. By remaining consistently and constantly the same as you move forward on the path to wealth accumulation, you will see the goal of your faith come to fruition.

Analyzing Your Financial Information

It is so important to know where you are before you can determine where you are going and what it is going to take to get you from point A to point B. Analyze your current financial situation in the following four categories. Then identify those areas that need to change in order for you to reach your goals.

It is so important to know where you are before you can determine where you are going and what it is going to take to get you from point A to point B.

---

1. Assets
2. Liabilities
3. Income
4. Outflow

The first category is your assets. This includes things such as your home, liquid cash, stocks and bonds, mutual funds, and personal property. Liabilities are those things that work against you financially such as credit-card debt, personal loans, investment loans, car loans and leases, and deferred income tax. Your income includes any you receive in the form of earned income from a job or business, income from rental property you own, investment income, a pension, and capital gains. Your outflow is your lifestyle expenditures such as mortgage payments, loan payments, rent, property taxes, maintenance costs, food and other household expenses, transportation, insurance premiums, discretionary spending, entertainment, and so on.

The strategy for wealth building is basically to create "extra," which is accomplished through increasing your income and/or decreasing your outflow. Anyone who can locate ways to do these two things can become wealthy. Identifying where you currently are, however, is critical. To give yourself a better picture of your financial profile, you will need to do two things. First, figure out your current net worth by listing the value of your assets and then subtracting your liabilities. The next thing you want to do is create a Household Cash-Flow Statement that lists your monthly income and monthly expenses. Most likely you will be able to locate areas in which your outflow is exceeding your income. Many times it is not until we actually put things in writing that we see where our money is going. You will probably be able to find a lot of "extra" that can be put toward your wealth-building goals and objectives.

Many times it is not until we actually put things in writing that we see where our money is going.

Write the Vision

Here are some worksheets to help you map out your financial goals and make them a reality:

Financial Goals Worksheet #1

Write down your short- and long-term goals. First list those things you would like to accomplish in the next three years and then write down your ten-year goals.

1. _____

2. _____

3. _____

4. _____

5. _____

6. _____

7. _____

8. _____

9. _____

10. _____

11. _____

12. _____

Top Five Goals

List your five most important goals and the specific things you can do to achieve them. Be as specific as possible when determining your action steps.

1. Goal: _____

   _____

   Action: _____

   _____

   _____

   _____

   _____

2. Goal: _____

   _____

   Action: _____

   _____

   _____

   _____

   _____

3. Goal: _____

   _____

   Action: _____

   _____

_____

_____

_____

4. Goal: _____

_____

Action: _____

_____

_____

_____

5. Goal: _____

Action: _____

_____

_____

_____

Prioritizing Your Financial Objectives

1. What are your current financial goals and objectives?

_____

_____

_____

_____

2. What are your most pressing financial concerns right now?

_____

_____

_____

_____

3. Are you anticipating any major lifestyle changes that could require money, e.g., retirement, inheritance, children going to college, a loved one needing care?

_____

_____

_____

_____

4. What is the best financial decision you have ever made?

_____

_____

_____

_____

5. What is the worst financial decision you have made?

_____

_____

_____

_____

6. Do you own any investments or real estate that you are planning to sell or want to sell in the near future?

_____

_____

_____

_____

7. Have you considered getting a financial advisor?

_____

_____

_____

_____

Creating a strong foundation for your financial plan requires solid biblical understanding, research and investigation, practical action, and the direction of the Holy Spirit. With these components in place, you can begin to refashion your financial thinking, decisions, and habits into a generational wealth context. An attitude of reverence for God's Word, combined with single-minded focus on expanding your financial capacity, is essential for achieving the highest levels of biblical prosperity. Assess where you are and start there. Commit to achieving your goals through diligence, discipline, and patience. You have been empowered by God to prosper, so lay hold of the wealth that rightfully belongs to you!

Commit to achieving your goals through diligence, discipline, and patience.

3

MANAGING BASIC ACCOUNTS

But thou shalt remember the Lord thy God: for it is he that giveth thee power to get wealth, that he may establish his covenant which he sware unto thy fathers, as it is this day.

—DEUTERONOMY 8:18

Every man also to whom God hath given riches and wealth, and hath given him power to eat thereof, and to take his portion, and to rejoice in his labour; this is the gift of God.

—ECCLESIASTES 5:19

Have you ever heard the saying, "You're so heavenly minded that you're no earthly good?" It is referring to the person who is spiritual but has no practical application of the Word of God in his or her life. We must combine the spiritual and the practical elements of the Bible in order to obtain the results we are expecting. As it pertains to finances, we cannot just quote Scripture all day long but fail to add corresponding action to our faith. The practical side of wealth building involves the key component of knowing how to manage basic accounts. This is essential to your plan to build generational wealth. If you know how to manage your accounts when your bank account balances are low, you will carry those good accounting habits into your wealthy place.

The practical side of wealth building involves the key component of knowing how to manage basic accounts.

Bank accounts are the equivalent to the "storehouses" mentioned in the Bible. These are essentially the places where you "store" your money. While there is nothing wrong with keeping some liquid cash at your disposal, either in your wallet or in your home, your bank accounts should be the place where the majority of your money is located. Different types of bank accounts can suit your needs, but everyone should start with the basics: a checking account and a savings account.

Believe it or not, many people don't have bank accounts. When they receive a paycheck, they go to a local check-cashing venue and pay a fee to have their checks cashed. Unfortunately, not having a checking account can actually be more costly in the long run. In addition to the money that you lose due to check-cashing fees, there is also the fact that people are more likely to spend money frivolously when cash is immediately at their disposal. This is just one of the many reasons why it is in our best interest to have a bank account. In addition, having an account enables us to "account" for our money and see exactly where it is going on a daily basis. Being a good steward over our finances is a key to God's releasing more into our lives.

Checking Accounts

A checking account allows you to put your money (checks, cash, money orders, and so on) into one account from which you can write checks, make deposits, or withdraw cash. You should have a checking account for many reasons, the first of which is protection. A checking account protects your money from theft, fire, or other events that can put your cash at risk. Second, having a checking account keeps you from having to carry cash around all the time and pay for things in cash. The convenience factor is one of the primary reasons why you want to have a checking account. It also enables you to take advantage of the direct-deposit feature, which you can set up through your employer. Direct deposit automatically deposits your paychecks into your account so you don't ever have to touch them or make a trip to the bank.

*The convenience factor is one of the
primary reasons why you want to have
a checking account.*

Of course fees are often associated with checking accounts, which you may avoid by adhering to certain guidelines a bank has for a particular account. For example, many banks will waive the monthly fee if you maintain a minimum balance in your bank account at all times, or if you have a minimum amount directly deposited into your account on a monthly basis. By establishing direct deposit, you can easily fulfill that requirement. Other banks offer free checking to college students. Some banks don't charge fees on their checking accounts at all. Do your research and find out where you can open an account that suits your needs.

There was a time when writing checks was the common way to pay for expensive purchases, or even to pay bills. Times have changed, however, and everything is really moving toward a completely paperless financial system. Because of this migration, banks offer customers *check cards* or *debit cards* as a convenience when opening a checking account. These are not credit cards but are used as electronic checks so you can make purchases by simply swiping your card for the amount charged to you. Check cards also allow you to withdraw money at ATMs as well as get cash back at the checkout line in the grocery store. They really are a convenience. Check cards typically have a Visa or MasterCard logo on them, as well as other ATM-friendly logos that enable you to use them virtually anywhere, from restaurants to the gas pump. You no longer have to carry cash with you. Instead, you can pay for things directly from your checking account.

If you have a checking account at any number of banks, you will notice that they give you the option of choosing to have your bank statements sent to you in the mail or electronically via e-mail. The same is true of bill collectors. Some people like to receive hard copies of their account statements and bills, while others find a constant pile of bills to be a waste of paper and a hassle. It is completely up to you what you prefer. Either way, you want to keep track of your bank account statements and records of your bills.

When using a checking account, it's important to remember the following things:

• You can't write a check for an amount that exceeds what is in your account. Doing so will result in a "bounced" check and will incur costly NSF (Not-Sufficient Funds) fees and penalties that can hurt your bank account balance. Writing bad checks can also raise red flags alerting banks that you are a customer who is a risk to them. You may even have your check-writing privileges revoked. Always be aware of what is in your account before writing a check or using your check card. If you have purchases that are pending and have not posted to your account, be sure to subtract those purchases from your balance so that you know the amount you are actually working with before making additional purchases.

• You may be required to keep a minimum balance in your account at all times. Again, this depends on the bank and the type of account you have.

• Balance your checkbook! You should know what is in your account at all times and where your money is going. Balancing your checkbook is one way to remain on top of your finances and never be caught off guard by a purchase you forgot to record. Even the little purchases add up over time. When you keep track of your purchases (checks, check card purchases, and withdrawals) you demonstrate good stewardship over your "storehouse."

• If you are still writing checks, don't write blank checks to people or companies and allow them to fill in the amount. Never let other people write checks for you.

• Always be sure to sign the back of a check that was written to you before cashing or depositing it in an ATM machine.

• Consider getting overdraft protection for your account. Utilizing this protection ensures that the money will be covered should you ever write a check or use your check card when there are insufficient funds in your account. Banks usually afford you overdraft protection by having you link a bank-issued credit card to your checking account that has a line of credit available. When your account goes into overdrawn status, the money is automatically transferred from the line of credit to your account, enabling you to avoid NSF fees. The amount that is transferred is added to your credit card balance and will show up on your credit card statement.

Balancing Your Checkbook Step-by-Step

Balancing your checkbook each month is a vital money-management step that will keep you on top of your finances. It will ensure that your records and bank statements agree with each other. Your check register is a component of your checking account that you should utilize each time you make a purchase. Here's how to balance your checkbook:

1. Look at your account statement. Take note of your beginning and ending balances. Also, pay attention to any interest earned and any monthly service or NSF fees that you incurred and add those to your check register.

2. Go through your check register and check off each item that is listed on your statement. Checking off an item means it has posted to your account or cleared the bank. You may also want to check off each item on your statement that you have checked off in your register. This will make it easier when you are trying to resolve an issue.

3. Check your statement for items that are listed there but you did not record in your register. Add any unlisted items to your register and check them off. Verify any unauthorized purchases or credits that you are not sure about with the bank.

4. List all the purchases that have not posted to your account in a separate column and total them up. This is the amount of your unreconciled debits.

5. List all of the unreconciled credits (deposits) to your account.

6. Take your ending balance that is on your statement and add the total of your outstanding credits to it. Then subtract the total of your outstanding debits from that amount. The number that you end up with should match the amount you have listed in your check register as your current balance.

7. If the numbers don't match, double-check your calculations.

8. Correct any mistakes you find and meet with a banking specialist, if necessary, to reconcile any discrepancies.

The Importance of Saving

There are plenty of reasons to open a savings account, some of which include building an emergency fund, preparing for a major purchase, earning additional interest, and laying a foundation for your long-term financial stability and generational wealth goals. But opening a savings account is just one step in your wealth-building plan. Saving is actually a lifestyle that involves discipline and focus. If your goal is to take your finances to the next level, you can grow your savings account in several ways.

A savings account is your personal financial "storehouse" and you should look at it as the account that you don't touch unless it is absolutely necessary. By "absolutely necessary," I mean an emergency or a situation in which you need the money immediately for something important that requires an amount you don't have in your checking account, such as a car repair. Outside of emergencies, you have to resolve in your mind that you *will not* touch the money in your savings account. If you spend what you are trying to save, it defeats the whole purpose.

A savings account is your personal financial "storehouse" and you should look at it as the account that you don't touch unless it is absolutely necessary.

One of the first things to realize about growing your account is that saving requires you to spend less, and spending less requires a mind-set change. The way you think determines the ultimate direction of your life, and your financial future depends on the way you think today. If you have the mind-set of hyper-consumption, then your finances will go in that direction. Habits you have practiced over the years are not undone overnight. We must continually renew our minds with the Word of God in order to align our thinking with God's plan for our lives.

Many times people feel they don't have the money to open a savings account, but that is not the issue at all. The issue is that they are overspending what they *do* have, which leaves them with nothing at the end of the month. Thankfully, resources available online and through your bank can enable you to track exactly how much you spend each month so you can make the necessary adjustments.

One of the biggest hindrances to saving is not getting in the habit of saving! It can be challenging to start a new habit that is foreign to you, especially when you have not developed the discipline to do it, but we all have to start somewhere. The first step is to get in the habit of paying yourself. You can do this by setting up automatic payments to your savings account the day you receive your paycheck (which you should have directly deposited into your checking account). Making everything automatic is the best way to start a savings routine. Be sure to record the transfer in your checkbook register as well.

One of the biggest hindrances to saving is not getting in the habit of saving!

Keep in mind that making excessive withdrawals from your savings account can backfire on you over time. Believe it or not, a federal regulation limits the number of withdrawals or transfers you can make from a savings account over the course of a month. When you go over that limit, the bank can charge you fees and penalties. This can severely cut into any interest your account may have accrued. For this reason, be mindful of savings withdrawals and, again, don't withdraw money unless it is an emergency.

When you have a nice amount in place, your savings account can also provide the benefit of being a source of overdraft protection for your checking account, which is probably a better option than a line of credit if you do not want a credit card. Having money in your savings account will provide a cushion for you in the event that a check bounces or the money in your checking account does not cover a transaction. This will help you avoid costly NSF fees. As with checking accounts, you must also research savings accounts in order to understand the details of the account you are considering. Find out if you must maintain a minimum balance and how many withdrawals you are allowed before you are penalized with fees.

Even if you start out saving ten dollars a month, it makes a difference. Your focus should be on developing new habits that position you for increase over time, and opening a savings account is a great way to do that.

Even if you start out saving ten dollars a month, it makes a difference.

CDs and Money Market Accounts

A CD is a *certificate of deposit,* also known as a *time deposit.* CDs are offered by banks and other financial institutions, such as credit unions, and are similar to savings accounts in that they are insured and thus virtually risk-free. The Federal Insurance Corporation (FDIC) insures banks, and the National Credit Union Administration (NCUA) insures credit unions. CDs differ from savings accounts in that the CDs have a specific, fixed term (often monthly, three months, six months, or one to five years) and, usually, a fixed interest rate. CDs are supposed to be held until they mature, at which time you may withdraw the money along with the interest it has accrued. In exchange for keeping the money for the agreed-upon term, institutions usually grant higher interest rates.

The accruing interest on a CD is what makes it an advantageous savings option. Fixed rates are common, but some institutions offer CDs with variable rates as well. Certificates of deposit typically require a minimum deposit, and may offer higher rates for larger deposits. You may receive a paper certificate that represents the CD, but since things are moving toward being completely paperless, your CD may simply be reflected on your bank statement.

Money Market Accounts

A money market account is another savings option available at your bank, but it is for people who have enough money to maintain the minimum balance. Typically, the interest rate on a money market account is higher than the rate on a basic savings account;

however, it is generally required that you maintain a *much* higher minimum balance than in a regular savings account. Some money market accounts require a minimum of anywhere from one thousand dollars to five thousand dollars, depending on the account. This is one of those accounts that you shouldn't open unless you are in the financial position to do so; otherwise, your money will not earn any interest and the bank will penalize you with fees.

Money market accounts do allow you to write checks on the account, but there is usually a limit on how many checks you can write in a given period of time. The financial institution also limits how many withdrawals you can make. While this account can be used as a checking account, it should be regarded more as a savings account than anything else. The good thing about being able to write checks or use a check card is that in emergency situations you don't have to go to an ATM to withdraw cash. The convenience of a money market account is that it has checking account features, while still functioning as a savings account. That is a bonus!

> *The convenience of a money market account is that it has checking account features, while still functioning as a savings account.*

Money market accounts are a great means with which to build an emergency savings fund. The higher interest rates are a smart savings component, and the limits to how many times you can withdraw money and write checks will help prevent you from dipping into your savings unnecessarily. Consider whether a money market account is right for you and inquire at your local banks about the money market accounts they have to offer.

If you haven't opened a checking and a savings account, now is the time to do it. Putting your money into the proper "storehouses" establishes a sense of order and organization in your financial life that will help you keep track of your money and develop discipline in how you manage it. Don't despise small beginnings! As you continue to demonstrate good stewardship over the money God brings into your hands, He will increase you over time. The financial practices you establish now will form a solid foundation that will sustain you as you move into your wealthy place.

Don't despise small beginnings!

THE BASICS OF INVESTING

Honour the LORD with thy substance, and
with the firstfruits of all thine increase:
So shall thy barns be filled with plenty,
and thy presses shall burst out with
new wine.

—PROVERBS 3:9–10

He that hath a bountiful eye shall be blessed;
for he giveth of his bread to the poor.

—PROVERBS 22:9

One of the ways to accomplish your goal of building wealth is to invest. For the beginner, it can be overwhelming to dive into the arena of investing, especially with so many different terms and options. Educating yourself about how to invest properly is important if you want to get involved. It can be lucrative or a bad idea, depending on how informed you are. If you do decide to include investing as one of your avenues to generational wealth, you need to know some things.

The most important rule of investing is this: Never invest money that you cannot afford to lose. Investing can be risky and often requires a financial advisor to help you make the best investment choices. Investing is essentially using your money to make more money, or allowing your money to work for you. It is very proactive, unlike saving, which is dealing more with securing the principal amount of money than with getting a return on the money. With investing, it is all about your returns. This is why it is so important to choose your investments wisely. A measuring stick used to determine the type of results you are likely to get from an investment is to look at the expected returns compared to the risks you anticipate.

Never invest money that you cannot afford to lose.

Keep in mind that both saving *and* investing should be incorporated into your wealth-building objectives; however, knowing the difference between the two is vital. One of the core investment options people choose is stocks. Some distinct characteristics about stock investing set it apart from saving. Three terms are usually associated with stocks: ownership, upside potential, and risk.

• Ownership: Buying stock is essentially buying a "piece" of a company, which makes you a part owner. As a co-owner, you have the right to vote on important issues pertaining to the stock-holding company as well as participate in profits if the dividends are distributed.

• Upside Potential: Participating in stock investing allows you to have a share in the company. It puts you in a position to reap the benefits of the investment as the value of the stock grows, which means more payout for you if the money is liquidated.

• Risk: When it comes to investing in stocks, you always have the risk of losing money. Some stocks have more risk than others, but with any investment vehicle, keep in mind that you can lose. This is why it is extremely important that you carefully consider investing in stocks before getting started. If the thought of losing money is something that frightens you or makes you uncomfortable, you may not be ready, or it may not be for you.

Here's what you have to take into consideration when deciding whether or not to invest. Saving gives you the guarantee that the five thousand dollars you put into your account is going to be there five years from now, possibly with a little gain from interest. With investing, you're dealing with potential, and you have to determine whether the *potential* gains that may come from investing that five thousand dollars is worth the risk of losing part of the money, or even all of it. Putting your money in a traditional savings account is a good route to take if you know you are definitely going to need those funds down the line. While saving and investing both involve your entrusting your finances to an organization, the end result is not always the same.

> *While saving and investing both involve*
> *your entrusting your finances to an organization,*
> *the end result is not always the same.*

What Is Stock?

Let's say you wanted to start up a clothing store or boutique with members of your family. In order to get your business up and running, you need $100,000, so you decide to incorporate a new company. You divide the company into one thousand pieces, or "shares" of stock. They are called "shares" because each piece of stock is entitled to a proportional share of the profit or loss. You assign a price of $100 to each new share. The goal is to sell all the shares to your family members so that you can acquire the $100,000 you need to start the business.

If the store earned $50,000 after taxes during its first year, each share of stock would be entitled to 1/1000th of the profit. You would take $50,000 and divide it by 1,000, which would result in $50 earnings per share. You could then call a meeting with the company's board of directors and decide to use the money to pay cash dividends, repurchase stock, or reinvest in the store.

Somewhere along the line, you may choose to sell your shares, and if the company is large enough you could opt to trade on a stock exchange. A stockbroker is someone who facilitates that process for you. You are essentially telling the market that you want to acquire or sell shares of a certain company, at which point Wall Street links you with someone and charges you a fee and commission. Regardless of where you invest your money, the principle of investing in shares of stock is the same: You are purchasing a small piece of the company.

There are two primary ways to make money from stocks. The first is from an *increase in the price of a share*. For example, if a business with a $10 stock price grew 20 percent over a ten-year period, it would be almost $62 per share within a decade. The second way you make money from stocks is from *dividends*. When earnings are distributed to you, the funds are now your property. Many people use this money to buy more stock.

Over time, studies have shown that owning stocks is one of the easiest and most profitable ways to acquire long-term wealth. Most millionaires and billionaires achieved their financial status by owning shares in public or private corporations, and so can you.

Mutual Funds

Mutual funds are another relatively easy and stress-free way to get involved with investing, and they are generally the most popular because they provide a way for the novice investor to buy a diversified portfolio of stocks, bonds, and other securities. There are mutual funds that match virtually every need and preference, from finding a place to store your temporary cash savings to earning dividends and capital gains on long-term global stocks. The convenience of mutual funds makes them a top pick for people who want to start investing.

*The convenience of mutual funds makes
them a top pick for people who want
to start investing.*

A mutual fund is basically a pool of money provided by individual investors, companies, and other organizations, and it consists of a few key components:

1. A board of directors or board of trustees.

   If the company is a corporation, the people who oversee it for the shareholders are known as *directors* and serve on a board of directors. If it is a trust, they are called *trustees* and serve on a board of trustees.

2. The cash, stocks, and bonds the fund holds.

3. Contracts.

   The fund itself has no employees, just contracts with other firms, which include custody (a bank that will hold all of the cash, bonds, stocks, or assets the fund owns in exchange for a fee), transfer agents (the people who keep track of your purchases and sales of the mutual-fund shares, and make sure you get your dividend checks, account statements, audit and accounting, etc.), and the investment management company that is paid a percentage of the assets in exchange for its services.

There are four basic types of mutual funds: closed-end, open-end, load, and no-load. Here is a more in-depth description of each:

1. Closed-End Funds

This type of mutual fund has a set number of shares issued to the public through an initial public offering. These shares trade on the open market; this, combined with the fact that a closed-end fund does not redeem or issue new shares like a normal mutual fund, subjects the fund shares to the laws of supply and demand. As a result, shares of closed-end funds normally trade at a discount to net asset value.

2. Open-End Funds

Most mutual funds are open-ended. This simply means that the fund does not have a set number of shares. Instead, the fund will issue new shares to an investor based on the current net asset value and redeem the shares when the investor decides to sell. Open-end funds always reflect the net asset value of the fund's underlying investments because shares are created and destroyed as necessary.

3. Load vs. No-Load

A load is a sales commission. If a fund charges a load, the investor will pay the sales commission on top of the net asset value of the fund's shares. No-load funds usually generate higher returns for investors due to the lower expenses associated with ownership.

Let's say you have fifteen thousand dollars to invest in a mutual fund. You would start the process by filling out an application for the fund (usually obtained on the company Web site) and mailing it in with the check for your initial investment. Your account would probably be open within a few days, at which point the following would take place:

1. You are issued shares of the mutual fund based on the value of the fund when your check was deposited.

2. The cash shows up in your account and will be visible to the portfolio manager who represents the advisor company. The manager will receive a report stating how much money is available to invest in additional stocks, bonds, or other securities based on the net money coming into or out of the fund.

3. When the portfolio manager is ready to buy shares of a stock, such as Coca-Cola, he or she will tell the trading department to make sure the order gets filled. The manager will work with stockbrokers, investment banks, and other sources of liquidity to find the stock and get his or her hands on it at the lowest possible price.

4. When the trade is agreed upon, the mutual fund will have the money taken out of the stock bank account on a settlement date and given to the person or institution that sold the shares of Coke to them in exchange for the Coke stock certificates, making the person or institution the new owner/custodian.

5. When Coca-Cola pays a dividend, it will send the money to the custodian, who will make sure it is credited to the mutual fund's account. The mutual fund will likely hold the money as cash so it can pay you a dividend at the end of the year.

*   *   *

Investing through a mutual fund is a great option if you want to take a more hands-off approach to the investment process. The investment manager who will be assigned to your account is trained in mutual-funds management and is able to devote the time and energy needed to select the best investments and oversee the account. This frees the investor from having to deal with the stress of analyzing statements and making calculations.

Each mutual fund will have a different investment strategy or purpose. For example, some invest only in blue-chip companies, while others choose to invest in new businesses or specific market sectors. The key is to locate what works best for you in an area that you are knowledgeable about. You don't want to invest in a company that deals in a field about which you have no knowledge or in which you have no interest. You need to research the companies and understand your investment.

To start investing in mutual funds, you can purchase fund shares just as you would a share of stock. You do this typically through a brokerage account. If you don't have a brokerage account, check out the fund's Web site or call the company to request information and an application. The minimum amount needed to start investing can range anywhere from $25 to $100,000.

Bonds

Another way to invest is through bonds. A bond is basically an IOU in which an investor agrees to loan money to a company in exchange for a predetermined interest rate. The company issues bonds at various interest rates and sells them to the public. Investors purchase the bonds with the understanding that the company will pay back the original amount plus any interest that is due by a set date (maturity date).

An investor benefits from a bond by receiving a check from the company at set intervals, depending on the contract. The rate of interest the bondholder earns depends on the strength of the corporation that issued the bond. An example of this would be a blue-chip company, which generally is more stable. A great tip to consider when investing in bonds is that generally, the higher the interest rate, the riskier the bond investment. Bonds may be issued by governments, municipalities, corporations, and other institutions.

Beware of Scams

Unfortunately, one of the downsides of investing is that there are many scams designed to fleece innocent investors and con them out of their money. These predatory practices and schemes are everywhere, which is why it is important never to jump into any type of investment without thoroughly researching the company and investment vehicle you are considering. Many people have lost money they can never recover because they didn't use wisdom, and they allowed the lure of a get-rich-quick scheme to deceive them. We must never allow a desire to be rich to navigate us down the wrong path. The Holy Spirit will always save you time, money, and energy, so pay attention to His voice.

We must never allow a desire to be rich to navigate us down the wrong path.

One investment scam that is prevalent is called a *Ponzi scheme* or *pyramid scheme*. It is an investment scam that promises high rates of returns on the investment. In a Ponzi scheme, the scam artist pools the funds received from the investors and actually lives off those funds himself, while paying a portion back to the investors as interest or gains. The scam artist supplies the unsuspecting victim with false documents or account statements that make it appear as if the investment is still intact and earning a high rate of return. The investors typically funnel more of their money into the scheme, often telling others about this great "opportunity."

What typically happens in this type of scheme is that the investors eventually begin to request the return of their original investment, plus its earnings, at which point the scam artists reach a point where they cannot collect enough new money to pay off the old investors. These schemes usually result in the authorities getting involved and are heartbreaking ordeals for the victims who invested their precious resources.

To avoid getting involved with scams that are designed to clean out your bank account, stick with legitimate companies and institutions as well as traditional investment vehicles such as stocks, bonds, mutual funds, real estate, etc. Never get involved with something that you have not done your homework on, or that looks or sounds suspicious in any way. If it seems too good to be true, it probably is.

If it seems too good to be true,
it probably is.

Other Ways to Invest

The great thing about investing is that there are many different options from which you can choose in order to give yourself a broad spectrum of investment vehicles. Consider the following:

1. Enroll in your company's 401(k) or 403(b) plan.

This is a basic investment maneuver that advisors generally recommend across the board. Most companies offer good investment options such as the 401(k) or 403(b) if you work for a nonprofit organization. These are great choices because you won't have to pay income taxes on the money, which allows your money to grow over time without the IRS taking a percentage. Keep in mind that withdrawing the funds prior to your retirement can result in penalties and fees. The 401(k) is simply an account in which you hold your investments such as stocks, bonds, and mutual funds; it is not the investment in and of itself.

2. Build an emergency savings account.

Have a goal to save at least one year's worth of money that you could live on if you were unemployed.

3. Consider a Roth IRA or traditional IRA.

Again, these are accounts that are used to hold investments like stocks, bonds, and so forth.

4. Purchase real estate.

Buying a home is one of the best investments you can make. Don't get stuck in the renting cycle. Begin putting money aside for a down payment on a home. Again, becoming a homeowner is a smart move because your home appreciates over time and builds equity.

If you are serious about building wealth, now is the time to start thinking about all the different avenues you can take to get on that path. You definitely want to put investing on your wealth-building to-do list. If you aren't in the position to invest yet, at least begin researching companies, institutions, and investment options that interest you and fit your goals. Gather as much information as you can so you will know what to do when you are ready to start. And if you are in a position to start investing, don't wait any longer! Take control of your financial future by getting involved with some of the key resources that are available to help your money grow. Your future is in your hands, and you can begin building generational wealth now by tapping into the wisdom of God on where to invest. When you get instructions from Him, step out in faith, knowing that your corresponding action will result in tangible results.

Your future is in your hands, and you can begin building generational wealth now by tapping into the wisdom of God on where to invest.

THE INTANGIBLES OF WEALTH BUILDING

5

Bring ye all the tithes into the storehouse,
that there may be meat in mine house, and
prove me now herewith, saith the LORD of hosts,
if I will not open you the windows of heaven, and
pour you out a blessing, that there shall not be
room enough to receive it. And I will rebuke the
devourer for your sakes, and he shall not destroy
the fruits of your ground; neither shall your vine
cast her fruit before the time in the field, saith
the LORD of hosts. And all nations shall call you
blessed: for ye shall be a delightsome land, saith
the LORD of hosts.

—MALACHI 3:10–12

When we talk about wealth-building strategies, some practical and spiritual elements need to be in place for us to reach the ultimate destiny of generational wealth God has for every Believer. Before getting into things like investing, saving, estate planning, and managing bank accounts, you need a spiritual foundation and understanding of the importance of obedience in giving financially to the kingdom of God. Jesus told us to seek first the kingdom of God and all other things would be added to our lives. Wealth is definitely a welcome "addition" to any person's life, but in order to prosper God's way we must be sure not to neglect the principle of seedtime and harvest, which includes planting the Word of God in our hearts so that we can grow a harvest of wealth. In addition, we must understand seedtime and harvest as it relates to being cheerful, willing, and obedient in our giving. This is an intangible wealth-building principle designed to move you into your wealthy place when activated.

We must understand seedtime and harvest
as it relates to being cheerful, willing,
and obedient in our giving.

Sowing and reaping are foundational principles that will never go away. *Seedtime and harvest* refers to every area of life, not just money. In the natural realm, seeds that are sown into the ground determine what type of crops will grow. For example, if a farmer sows corn seeds into the ground, he is sure to receive a harvest of corn. Likewise, when you sow the seed of God's Word in your heart, it is inevitable that you will reap His promises. Before you see manifestation of wealth in your life, you have to sow wealth "seed" in your heart.

The Word of God is referred to as "incorruptible seed" that comes from God, which means that it will never fail. Your heart is the "ground" for sowing. When you decide what kind of harvest you want, you can find out what kind of seed you need to sow based on the Word of God. As it relates to wealth, you will have to start the process by allowing the Word to take root in your heart. You do this by finding Scriptures pertaining to prosperity and then meditating on them constantly. Speaking the Scriptures on prosperity is also a way to plant them within your spirit. As you continue to read, confess, and meditate on the Word constantly, you will begin to find an image of wealth growing inside you. By keeping the Word before you at all times, you cultivate a prosperity mind-set that will begin to shape your decisions, ultimately taking you in the direction of generational wealth.

A Complete Definition of Prosperity

True prosperity is the ability to meet the needs of mankind in any realm of life. As it relates to the financial realm, we want to position ourselves for wealth so that we can not only enjoy it ourselves but help meet the needs of others. This is God's number-one covenant purpose for making us rich in material goods and resources. Several things about prosperity fall under the intangible category:

True prosperity is the ability to meet the needs
of mankind in any realm of life.

---

1. Prosperity starts in a person's soul (3 John 2).
2. Prosperity involves excelling to the place desired.
3. Prosperity means making good progress in the pursuit of anything desired.
4. True prosperity will always go away from selfishness and extend toward others.
5. Prosperity is an inward attitude, not just an outward gathering of possessions.
6. Prosperity deals with every area of life: spirit, soul, and body.

Many people are rich in material possessions, but when it comes to their relationships with others, they leave much to be desired. Similarly, what good is it to be financially wealthy and rich in "things" but dying of an incurable disease? You see, true wealth originates in the heart and mind of a person, and so does prosperity. It is God's will that we obtain wealth, but we must allow the image of prosperity to take root in our hearts and minds and work its way to the outside. The Word *is* the spiritual seed of prosperity, which plants the image of prosperity inside us when we meditate on it day and night.

The use of the word *prosperity* has evolved over time. In the original Hebrew, it was used as a parting utterance between people. The original definition means "to be on the right path and have a successful journey in life." God wants Christians to have a prosperous journey in life (Genesis 24:21; Romans 1:10), and part of that journey involves being in a position financially to bless others and future generations. Over time, the word *prosperity* changed to mean success in profitability and material gain, and this is primarily how the world sees it. *Prosperity*, however, should now be used to mean wholeness and continued well-being in every area of life. Believers should be reflections of prosperity in their health, relationships, careers, *and* bank accounts.

Believers should be reflections of prosperity in their health, relationships, careers, and bank accounts.

Understand that money is just a by-product of prospering in God. Money was never meant to be the sum total of the word *prosperity*. It is possible to be financially rich and be poor in other areas of life, as I mentioned. However, true prosperity in the life of a Believer will summon whatever is needed from God in any situation (2 Corinthians 9:8).

Unlocking the Combination for Prosperity

There is a sequence that can be used for living the prosperous life. The first principle in this sequence is to understand God's system of operation. Wealth acquisition does not just happen because we want it to, or because we read in the Word that God will prosper us. The intangibles are just as important as the practical things we must do to position ourselves for wealth and financial increase. Christians must make seeking and researching God's way of doing things their priority to gain understanding (Matthew 6:33). God has a purpose for the wealth He brings into our lives. We are not just to consume it in our own selfish desires. Everything God does has a purpose, and when we don't understand the purpose, abuse is inevitable. With that being said, Believers must know that their primary allegiance is to the kingdom of God, which means we have to know how to function in this kingdom. We must grab hold of this in order to prove that true, godly prosperity in the form of wealth and riches is obtainable.

I want to revisit the issue of sowing and reaping because this is the foundation of the kingdom of God. Mark 4:1–33 records the parable of the sower, in which Jesus likens the kingdom to the way a farmer sows seed in the ground. He describes the different types of "soil" in people's hearts and how the condition of that soil can determine the type of results each person gets from the seed sown of God's Word.

For example, in farming, you have a farmer; in the kingdom of God, you have a "sower." In farming you have to have seed; in the kingdom of God, the Word is the seed. In farming you have to have good ground in order to provide a fertile environment in which the seed can grow; in the kingdom of God, the ground is the heart of a man. In farming you have to have a method of planting seed; in the kingdom of God, the method of planting seed is to speak the Word of God. In farming, fruit grows; in the kingdom of God, the fruit that grows is called "life." In farming, and in the kingdom of God, there has to be a harvester—a person who receives the benefit of planting the seed. We cannot expect to receive anything from the kingdom of God without respecting this process of spiritual "farming" that God has implemented in order for His people to get results. Accessing wealth and riches is no different.

In farming, fruit grows; in the kingdom of God, the fruit that grows is called "life."

When the soil of a man's heart receives the seed of God's Word, conception has taken place. If wealth and riches are the harvest you want to see in your life, you have to start with Word-seed. The manufacturing center for prosperity is on the inside of a man, according to Luke 17:21, which says, "Neither shall they say, Lo here! Or, lo there! For, behold, the kingdom of God is within you." The degree to which a person sows seed in his or her heart is going to determine the harvest that is received. A Christian who is constantly confessing the Word of God where financial prosperity is concerned is sowing much seed, while a person who speaks negatively or says things to foster a poverty mentality will not operate in the hundredfold return. Whenever you speak negatively, you create a conflict between the good and bad seed that is in your heart. But the person who skillfully uses words and sets his or her will to confess only the Word of God will operate in tremendous financial prosperity. This is because only the right seed is being planted, which will later produce results.

The second step in the sequence of unlocking prosperity is developing in the love of God. This is another one of those intangible spiritual principles that translates into tangible gains. Developing in the love of God builds your character and puts you in a position where God can trust you with financial wealth.

Immature Believers, who refuse to develop God's love in their lives and are more focused on money than God, will not prosper. The kingdom of God is a kingdom of love, and developing God's character is *essential* to your prosperity.

The kingdom of God is a kingdom of love, and developing God's character is essential to your prosperity.

In Matthew 22:37–40 Jesus sets forth a new law that He says sums up all the laws of the Old Testament: "Thou shalt love the Lord thy God with all thy heart, and with all thy soul, and with all thy mind. This is the first and great commandment. And the second is like unto it, Thou shalt love thy neighbor as thyself. On these two commandments hang all the law and the prophets." It is not enough to have a mental knowledge of the love of God; you must choose to develop in the character of love. This involves being a person of integrity and making the right decisions in the midst of difficult situations. When you make decisions in line with love, you develop the right character.

It is dangerous to refuse to develop in your love walk as a Believer. Too many wonderful things are on the line to allow things like hurt, unforgiveness, bitterness, and strife to dictate your responses to people and situations. God has an inheritance for each and every Believer, and that inheritance includes generational wealth and riches. But in order to meet the requirements of love, you have to mature in your love walk. You do this by choosing the love route rather than the flesh route. You must understand, think, and speak love in order to be considered a mature Christian.

*It is dangerous to refuse to develop in
your love walk as a Believer.*

God is not going to put financial wealth, supernatural power, and increase in the hands of spiritual babies because money is an amplifier. Whatever character issues you have in your life will only be brought to the forefront even more. If selfishness rules your life, and God and other people aren't your priorities, then the money you do have will only be squandered on your lusts, and it could ultimately destroy you. Kingdom prosperity is insulated with the love of God: love for God first, and then love for others.

It is incorrect to believe that God does not want His people to be wealthy. Many Christians, unfortunately, have not heard the Word of God preached about biblical finances, so they mistakenly believe that going without and experiencing financial lack are the will of God for their lives. Many even believe that poverty makes them humble. Nothing is further from the truth. Poverty doesn't make you humble; it makes you desperate for resources. What God *is* concerned with is that we don't seek to be rich more than we seek Him. The person who truly prospers and attains the level of generational wealth God has designed for him or her will be a lover of God first and foremost (Psalm 122:6).

Since God puts such a great emphasis on developing in the character of love, what does it mean to love God with all your "strength," as Luke 10:27 states? To love God with your strength means to love Him with your possessions, abilities, anointing, influence, power, and money. In other words, whatever you have that can be used to make a difference in people's lives is to be used to love God. Mark 10:17–22 gives the account of a rich young ruler whom Jesus invited to follow Him at the cost of selling all his possessions. This young man was immature in his love for God. Instead of being willing to sell his things and give the money to the poor, he left Jesus' presence with a heavy heart. Unfortunately, he loved his possessions more than he loved God, even though he was well versed in the law of Moses. Those who fail to make God their strength will satisfy their own selfishness through possessions. When we love God with our possessions, however, we put ourselves in position to prosper as never before.

The third step in the process of unlocking wealth in your life is to depart from iniquity and maintain a pure heart. Second Timothy 2:19, 22 says, "Nevertheless the foundation of God standeth sure, having this seal, The Lord knoweth them that are his. And, Let every one that nameth the name of Christ depart from iniquity...Flee also youthful lusts: but follow righteousness, faith, charity, peace, with them that call on the Lord out of a pure heart."

A person's heart is pure when it is free from anything that will defile or corrupt it. Having a pure heart is essential to possessing wealth and maintaining an inflow of financial prosperity. To be pure means to be unpolluted, genuine, uncontaminated, and free from anything sinister or underhanded. Purity is the gateway to success and life in the realm of the supernatural. It guarantees a life of manifestation.

> *A person's heart is pure when it is free from anything that will defile or corrupt it.*

Elisha's servant Gehazi is an example of a man who was corrupted by an impure heart due to a spirit of greed. The prophet Elisha had refused to accept Naaman's gifts, but Gehazi went behind Elisha's back and received them even though the Lord had not instructed Elisha to do so. Gehazi lied for his own selfish gain, and as a result, he was afflicted with leprosy.

Trying to plant the Word-seed of prosperity in an impure heart is futile and will not produce results. Deliverance comes to those with pure hands and hearts. The Word of God is a rod of power that, when wielded by a Believer in faith and integrity, will cause manifestation. Those who have pure hearts position themselves for the blessing of God to operate in their lives. You can develop in purity by obeying the truths found in God's Word. The Christian who desires to be like Jesus will purify his or her life.

Meditating on the Word of God is critical to unlocking prosperity in your life. Meditation is an intense study of the Word that you do by considering, speaking, and uttering the Scriptures on a regular basis. It is a process that involves the eyes, ears, and mouth. Focused consideration of what God has said about wealth and riches being His will for your life will cause that truth to be rooted in your heart. To meditate on God's Word is to respect the kingdom of God system and His way of doing things. It is a way to actively engage the seedtime and harvest process.

> *Meditating on the Word of God is critical*
> *to unlocking prosperity in your life.*

Joshua's success was based on his observance of the Word of God (Joshua 1:7–8). Ultimately, his commitment to meditate intensely by keeping the Word in his mouth and before him at all times was responsible for his victory. By meditating on the Word, you will understand what to do to prosper in life. You will be rooted in the will of God and flourish in the financial arena.

We cannot overlook the importance of obtaining faith as a seed in order to activate the blessings of wealth in our lives. Everything in the kingdom of God operates by faith, which means that without faith it is impossible to please God or prosper His way. You have to *believe* God wants you to prosper! The Word of God contains the faith of God, and faith in your heart gives birth to confidence. The degree of confidence a person has determines the level of his or her harvest.

The Word is the gateway to the manifestation of all wealth and Believers must begin to plan their harvests by planting the seed of God's Word in their hearts, long before it is needed. If you want your financial future to look a certain way, plant the seed for it now! Faith will increase as you continue to meditate on and speak God's Word.

If you want your financial future to look a certain way, plant the seed for it now!

Giving: A Corresponding Action to Your Faith

Faith without works is dead, which means that unless your faith has corresponding action behind it, it is nonproductive. Giving is a corresponding action that coincides with faith for obtaining wealth and riches. You may have heard the phrase, "I make my living through my giving." For the Christian, this is how we live. We do not toil and sweat to make money, but we commit to operating the principle of seedtime and harvest where our giving is concerned.

Giving financially into the kingdom of God is a corresponding action that is supposed to be birthed out of love. God is not as much concerned about the dollar amount of our offering as He is about the condition of our hearts when we give. He is also looking at what we give in proportion to what we have. For someone who already has a million dollars in the bank, a thousand-dollar offering is not a big sacrifice. It doesn't really require the individual to stretch his or her faith. But to a person who has only three hundred dollars in the bank, a thousand-dollar offering would be quite a leap of faith if the money came into his or her hands.

We should never give under compulsion or out of tradition. Giving like that is mechanical and devoid of power because it doesn't come from the heart. When we give with motives other than the fact that we love God and we want to honor Him with our "strength," which includes our finances, our giving is not going to produce the desired results. God is looking at our hearts, not simply the dollar amount we give. He is looking to see if people are cheerful, joyous, and quick to obey when He instructs them in this area.

God is looking at our hearts, not simply the dollar amount we give.

I remember the first time the Lord told me to give a large sum of money in an offering. I thought, Was that me, God, or the devil speaking? First of all, the devil is never going to tell you to give anything to the kingdom of God. It wasn't me because I personally did not *want* to give that amount at the time. I realized it was God speaking to me and even though my flesh was screaming, I obeyed Him. Since then I have become confident in the principle of seedtime and harvest because I have seen the results that come as a result of being obedient with my finances. Everything that God has called my wife and me to do, He has also provided the resources for, because we are faithful to put corresponding action to our belief that God will supply all of our needs, no matter what they are. The financial blessings I have experienced in my life are largely due to my commitment to be a giver, and I can honestly say, like Abraham, that no man made me rich but God.

There are four levels of giving that we must get involved with as Christians. They are:

1. Tithing.
2. Freewill offerings.
3. Kingdom demand offerings.
4. Firstfruit offerings.

Tithing is our covenant connection to the blessing of God. To "tithe" something means to give 10 percent of it. In actuality, the tithe *belongs* to God anyway, so when we receive financial increase, we are paying our tithes back to Him. Again, tithing is not something we do out of fear or with a law-based mentality. It is simply Believers saying to God that we are grateful for how He has blessed us financially and we are honoring Him with 10 percent of all our increase. Anytime we give something to God from a pure heart, a spiritual exchange takes place. God blesses obedience and He blesses honor. When we tithe, we take part in a system that is designed to empower us to prosper (Malachi 3:10).

God blesses obedience and He blesses honor.

Now please understand that when you give your tithe in church, God does not physically take your money; however, what He does receive is your love and honor for Him. Anything you do for God is rewarded in one way or another. Tithing is an act of faith and trust, especially when the temptation comes to spend the tithe on something else. I have been a tither for many years, and I can testify to the goodness of God (as well as the protection) that comes as a result of honoring God with 10 percent of my financial increase. It is the spiritual financial foundation that lays the groundwork for the other levels of kingdom giving.

Freewill offerings are tokens of appreciation for God's goodness in your life (Psalm 126:6). After the tithe, the next step is to give offerings. Again, the motive should always be love for God, not a sense of obligation. Second Corinthians 9:7 in *The Amplified Bible* says, "Let each one [give] as he has made up his own mind and purposed in his heart, not reluctantly or sorrowfully or under compulsion, for God loves (He takes pleasure in, prizes above other things, and is unwilling to abandon or to do without) a cheerful (joyous, "prompt to do it") giver [whose heart is in his giving]."

Notice a few key things in this passage. First, what makes a freewill offering effective is that it is something the giver has purposed in his or her heart to do, meaning there is a sense of fixed purpose and conviction about the amount of the offering. It is not something the person was pressured to do but something he or she alone decided. This person is settled in his or her decision to give. It is not something that is done reluctantly—outwardly giving the money but inwardly cringing and wishing he or she didn't have to. God looks at the attitude in which we give, and when we give from our hearts, cheerfully and with excitement, it gives God pleasure. This is the characteristic of freewill offerings that makes them a powerful tool in the kingdom of God system of seedtime and harvest.

Kingdom demand offerings are given when God speaks to you to give a specific amount in order to sow into something kingdom-related. Your church may be starting a new project or outreach that requires finances to get the job done. God may speak to you to sow a certain amount into the project. Or He may tell you to give to an organization or mission objective. Whenever He tells you to give a certain amount, it is for a reason. Trust and obey Him in this area because it is designed only to position you to receive more from Him. This is especially important to understand as you move into generational wealth, where God will be counting on you to help finance kingdom objectives in the earth on a large scale.

> *Whenever He tells you to give a certain amount,*
> *it is for a reason.*

The fourth level of kingdom giving is firstfruit offerings. The firstfruit offering is the first and best of our increase. Proverbs 3:9–10 tells us to honor the Lord with the firstfruits of all our increase so that our households will be filled with plenty. A firstfruit offering would be, for example, if you received a raise on your job of five hundred dollars. The first paycheck you get that reflects an increase due to the raise would be an opportunity to give that amount as a firstfruit offering. In other words, it is a one-time offering that you give when you receive the *first* increase to your paycheck.

In addition to giving, we must also continue to work, trust God, wait patiently, and thank Him in advance for our financial prosperity and increase. The path to wealth accumulation involves a process of spiritual and practical steps that work cohesively to produce maximum results. Grasping the intangibles is mandatory because everything in the natural realm proceeds from the activation of spiritual laws and principles. Love, integrity, and honor are three keys to wealth and riches that you must use to unlock the promises of God in your life. As you grow in these areas and

simultaneously use the wisdom of God in practical money mat-
ters, the covenant of wealth will become a reality in your life.

*Love, integrity, and honor are three keys to wealth
and riches that you must use to unlock the promises
of God in your life.*

6

WEALTH-BUILDING STRATEGIES

For where your treasure is, there will your
heart be also.

—MATTHEW 6:21

Thus saith the LORD, thy Redeemer, the Holy One
of Israel; I am the LORD thy God which teacheth
thee to profit, which leadeth thee by the way that
thou shouldest go.

—ISAIAH 48:17

One of the reasons people fail in their endeavors to gain ground financially is because they do not plan for wealth. This is a concept that doesn't involve just one component, such as saving or investing. Preparing for wealth involves having a detailed outline of how you plan to achieve your objectives. It is a multifaceted approach that incorporates different components to reach your goal. Having a financial advisor is definitely a piece of the wealth-building puzzle, and you should consider bringing one on board to help you really get on the right track. It is critical, however, that you ask the right questions and follow some general guidelines before you make your final selection.

Preparing for wealth involves having a detailed outline of how you plan to achieve your objectives.

Keep in mind that you don't *have* to get a financial manager; many people go it alone and are able to achieve their objectives. You can look at a financial manager in the way you do a mechanic. When something is wrong with your car, you can try to make the repair yourself, but if you take your car to a certified technician, you are more likely to get the problem solved and avoid making costly mistakes in the process. A financial advisor is similar to that car repair technician in that he or she is trained in proven financial management techniques. The truth is, understanding how to manage the financial arena takes lots of research, effort, and time. Most people do not have the time to learn all the details of financial management. In addition, you have developed habits and behaviors over time that you need to revamp, and there is information that you simply don't know. You can reach your goal much quicker when you have someone knowledgeable working with you and keeping you disciplined and on track. This is why having a financial advisor is beneficial.

When considering someone to help guide your financial affairs, you want to make sure you find a person who is truly qualified to handle them. Honesty, integrity, and a genuine understanding of the financial arena are essential. You want to choose someone with whom you can develop a good rapport and trust. The wrong person can turn out to be a disaster, so do your research and take your time locating a financial advisor who is right for you.

Honesty, integrity, and a genuine understanding of the financial arena are essential.

Finding the Right One

Credentials are of the utmost importance when choosing a financial advisor. Anyone can call him- or herself a financial planner. For this reason, you always want to make sure he or she is recognized as a CFP (certified financial planner), a CPA/PFS (certified public accountant/personal financial specialist) or a ChFC (chartered financial consultant). You don't want to assume, however, based on the advisor's certification alone that you're guaranteed to get the right advice. It is also a great idea to get referrals. Close friends and family members who have worked with a particular advisor will give you peace of mind, so ask those in your immediate circle if they know of a good CFP they can refer you to.

You also want to choose someone who has proven experience, particularly in the financial arena that matches your current age and stage of life. For example, a twenty-year-old college student may have different objectives from someone with children or someone in his or her retirement years. Find out what services are offered and if those services match your needs. Two great resources for finding certified financial planners are the National Association of Personal Financial Advisors (NAPFA) and the Garrett Planning Network. As with all CFPs, you will pay a fee in order to use their services, though some organizations may charge more or less than others, and some charge on an hourly basis.

Here are some other things to consider when choosing a CFP:

- **Consider the planner's pay structure.** Try to avoid planners or advisors who work on commission. Because their incentive is to get as much commission as possible, they may push certain products on you more aggressively, whether or not they are the best products for you. It is best to get an advisor who charges by the hour, especially if you are just looking for the basics and have pretty simple objectives as a beginner. Typically, advisors who charge an hourly fee are in the beginning stages of building their business and will need your recommendation, so they will be concerned with handling things in the best way possible.

- **Look for a fiduciary.** This advisor has a legal and ethical responsibility to act on behalf of the client at all times. Financial planners who are fiduciaries are held to higher standards and will be sure to give you advice and steer you in the direction of products that are tailor-made to fit your needs versus trying to sell you something just to make a profit.

- **Run a background check.** You need to find out if this person has ever been convicted of a crime and whether or not any regulatory body or investment-industry group has ever put him or her under investigation. Once you run a background check, ask the advisor for client references from those who have the same objectives and goals you do. Also, do your research to see if he or she has ever received disciplinary action for any unlawful or unethical practices during his or her professional career. Check to see if the advisor is registered with the state or the US Securities & Exchange Commission. Also, the planner must be able to provide you with a disclosure form called Form ADV Part II or the state equivalent of that form. Visit www.cfp.net for more information.

- **Verify the person's credentials.** The financial industry, by nature, is a prime arena where people have a tendency not to operate in the highest levels of integrity. When it comes to your money, you want to make sure the person you are bringing on board is on top of his or her game when it comes to his or her presentation. Take time to Google the person and check to see who administers the designation. Follow up with a phone call to the designator to verify that the credentials of your potential CFP are valid.

- **Ask about his or her philosophy.** An advisor's philosophy will dictate his or her approach to the field. Find out how the planner's personal philosophy regarding finances and helping others translates to his or her practice.

- **Beware of "market-beating" claims.** Don't buy into an advisor's predictions or claims of market-beating performance. *No one* can guarantee it. What you do want to hear is that he or she will give you good, sound advice about a variety of financial objectives, including, but not limited to, investing.

- **Ask the CFP if he or she will be the only person working with you.** The financial planner may work with you personally, or he or she may be your main contact while another team member works with you more closely.

- **How will you pay for the CFP's services?** Know the financial planner's fees before you finalize your decision. Typically, fees are charged in one of three ways: 1) fee-only, meaning that all fees are paid by the client, with no commissions; 2) commissions, which means payments are based on the products sold to you; or 3) salary, meaning the advisor is paid from the commissions you pay the company. Always ask what the person typically charges and get an estimate for the services you need.

- **Ask for a written agreement that details the services that he or she will provide to you.**

Pros and Cons of Online Trading

As you navigate the world of financial goal setting, you will find so many options and avenues you can take to get to your ultimate destination of wealth. One of those avenues is online trading. This allows you to engage in the investment process without having to go through a broker or a financial advisor. It saves you time and money, which is why many people choose this route. Before the Internet, investing and trading stocks meant following the newspaper or a cable channel and then calling a broker to make a trade. Today, online trading companies allow you to trade stocks from the comfort of your home, so it really is a convenience. But there are some pros and cons to trading online.

One of the pros of online trading is the fact that the Internet is at your disposal while you trade, so you can get information about the stocks you are looking at immediately. You can search the company Web site or do a general search for the company you want to invest in to see what is being said about it. As an Internet user, you are not limited to a specific time of day to get the information you need. You can also trade instantaneously if you want. The speed the Internet affords you can make the difference between winning and losing. When you use an online trading company, its overhead is typically low, so the fee structure is also generally lower. Since there is no broker to deal with, you won't have anyone trying to convince you not to make a trade. You can buy stocks as you please without any outside opinions to sway your decisions.

> *The speed the Internet affords you can make the difference between winning and losing.*

As with anything, there are also disadvantages. One disadvantage is that you do not have the assistance and support of an experienced broker. If you are a novice investor, having an experienced professional in your corner is especially beneficial. You may be just starting out and are not knowledgeable about stock trading or what stocks are best to choose. This is where a broker can be of great assistance. In addition, a broker who works for a bigger company has access to more information relating to the international market, whereas some online trading companies may not be able to accommodate overseas trading, if you desire to do that.

Another drawback to any online service is that technology can fail at any given time. You may want to make a trade but the Web site is down or inaccessible for some reason. Time is of the essence when dealing with stocks, and anything that slows your ability to trade in a quick and efficient manner can decrease your profits. While the Internet is a wonderfully useful and resourceful tool, glitches do happen, which can affect your results.

These are some of the things you should take into consideration when making a decision on how and where you want to invest. ShareBuilder is an online investment option that allows you to customize your investment portfolio. Other online trading firms include Charles Schwab and Scottrade.

As with any financial decision, never neglect God in the process. He wants to be involved every step of the way and when you seek the Holy Spirit for wisdom, you will never go wrong. He will save you time, money, and energy, and He will direct you to the financial manager who is the right fit for you. Whether you choose to invest in stocks through an online trading company, hire a financial manager, or go it alone, God's guidance, combined with practical expressions of your faith, will always lead you to prosperity.

As with any financial decision, never neglect
God in the process.

ESTATE PLANNING: WISDOM FOR YOUR FUTURE

Wealth and riches shall be in his house: and his righteousness endureth for ever.

—PSALM 112:3

Have you ever thought about what would happen to your belongings and property after you die? Most people don't like to think about this because it forces them to come to grips with the inevitable reality of death. While we do release our faith for a long, strong, healthy life, we should always attend to the practical, natural aspects as well when it comes to our finances. One of the things essential to a solid wealth-building plan is estate planning. It ensures that the assets you have acquired over the years are secured after you pass and places them in the care of those you designate. It allows you to leave a legacy of wealth to your children and grandchildren and through your specific designations, you can make sure that the things you have worked hard to achieve are not squandered or lost. Estate planning is a wise financial decision that everyone should take the time to make.

One of the things essential to a solid wealth-building plan is estate planning.

Estate planning is the process of anticipating and arranging for the disposal and disbursement of an estate and/or all of your assets after you die. Estate planning typically attempts to eliminate uncertainties over who gets what. Most people know that the most stressful post-death concerns involve the financial assets and estate of the deceased. If the deceased did not make arrangements or engage in estate planning, the situation can quickly spiral into confusion between family members and lead to serious issues. Families have been divided over the financial and legal issues surrounding a deceased loved one who never designated where the money and property would go after his or her death.

Elements of Estate Planning

There are several elements of estate planning that you should know. Familiarize yourself with the terminology so that you can be ahead of the game. Even if you are not anticipating your death anytime soon, it is a good idea to begin this process so you don't have to worry about it later. Here are some pointers as you begin the process of planning your estate:

- Your net worth is not a criterion for establishing an estate plan. Plan ahead regardless of your current financial status.

Some people think they shouldn't bother with estate planning because they don't have any real assets or possessions of significant value. Regardless of your net worth, you should still have a plan in place. This ensures that your financial goals and objectives are carried out after you die, and it involves your family in that process. You may not have many assets now, but that does not mean you won't when you die. If anything, planning ahead will put your goals in focus and remind you to continue pressing toward your financial objectives for acquiring wealth and riches while you are still here.

- Consider the different elements of your estate plan.

The elements of estate planning you should learn about include a will, power of attorney, medical power of attorney, and a living will or trust. Also included in the elements of estate planning is the specifying of final arrangements: where and how you would like to be buried (or cremated). Estate planning is a benefit because it maximizes the value of the estate by reducing taxes and other expenses. Always inform yourself of the federal and state laws that apply to your situation and govern yourself accordingly.

- Take inventory of your assets.

Your assets include your investments, any and all savings accounts, insurance policies, and real estate. When making the decision as to who will be the beneficiary of your assets, ask yourself three questions: Whom do I want to inherit my assets? Whom would I want to handle my financial affairs if I ever became incapacitated? Whom do I trust to make critical medical decisions for me if I am not in a position to make them for myself? Take time to really think about these questions and be deliberate in your final answers. Talk to your heirs and communicate your wishes clearly to them. The sooner you handle this, the less likely it is that disputes will occur once you are gone. You want to make sure that your assets are in good hands after you die.

Sometimes certain family members may not be ones to whom you can entrust your estate. Be honest with yourself. You may have children who you know are not responsible or likely to handle things the way you would want them handled. The key is to leave your legacy in the hands of someone who is trustworthy and responsible, and who understands the value of the financial foundation you have laid.

Be honest with yourself.

- Be mindful of laws governing estate planning.

The laws governing estate planning are not set in stone, which means that you need to stay abreast of any changes in current laws. For example, the Tax Relief Act of 2001 made changes that involve increases in state tax exemption and a revision in how the taxes on inherited assets are calculated. You will want to have an estate-planning attorney on your team to help you plan in the most financially advantageous way and protect your assets. Having a lawyer is also a great way to stay current with changing laws.

- Make a will.

A will is the staple of your estate plan. It spells out in very specific terms exactly where you want your assets to go. If you don't have one, a court will decide who gets your assets. In your will, you name a guardian for your children (if you have them) as well as take care of any assets outside of your trust. Not having a will can prove to be extremely costly and stressful to your family members and can also put your assets in the hands of people you would never approve to handle them. Family members who don't have a will to abide by can easily get into drawn-out disputes that turn into full-blown battles. Don't neglect this vital part of your estate plan. Keep in mind that you can amend your will at any point in time. You should review your will regularly and make any necessary changes as time progresses.

*You should review your will regularly
and make any necessary changes
as time progresses.*

You also want to make sure you have what is known as a "pour-over" will, which ensures that all the assets you intended to put into your trust are put there, even if you fail to retitle them before your death. A *living will* is a statement that specifies your wishes for the type of life-sustaining medical intervention you want, if any, in the event that you become terminally ill and/or unable to speak for yourself. You will want to assign medical *power of attorney* to an individual you trust to make critical medical decisions for you if you become incapacitated. This person should understand important medical information related to your treatment, be able to make sound decisions under pressure, and always have your best interests in mind when making those decisions. If you become incapacitated without having a power of attorney assigned, the court will intervene and appoint someone as guardian. This can be costly, so it is in your best interest to designate someone ahead of time.

• Establish a trust.

A trust is a legal mechanism that allows you to put conditions on how and when your assets will be distributed after you die. It also allows you to minimize gift and estate taxes, which is a plus. Trusts typically deal specifically with certain assets such as life insurance and real estate, but not the sum total of your holdings.

A trust is a beneficial component of your estate plan if you have a net worth of at least $100,000 and meet one of the following conditions:

1. The majority of your assets are in real estate, a business, or an art collection.

2. You want to leave your estate to your heirs in a way that is not directly payable to them when you die. For example, you may specify that they receive their inheritance in incremental amounts over specific time periods rather than in a lump sum all at once.

3. You want to support your surviving spouse but also ensure that the remainder of your estate goes to the designated heirs after your spouse dies.

4. You and your spouse want to maximize your estate-tax exemptions.

5. You have a disabled relative whom you would like to provide for without disqualifying him or her from government assistance.

The primary advantages of trusts are:

1. They allow you to put conditions on how and when your assets are distributed after your death.

2. They reduce estate and gift taxes.

3. They distribute assets to heirs in an efficient manner without probate costs.

4. They protect your assets from creditors and lawsuits.

5. They name a successor trustee, who manages the trust after you die.

A basic trust plan may cost anywhere from $1,600 to $3,000 or more, depending on the type of trust you get. These plans vary and can be complex. The five standard forms of trusts are:

1. Credit-shelter trust.

2. Generation-skipping trust.

3. Qualified personal residence trust.

4. Irrevocable life insurance trust.

5. Qualified terminable interest property trust.

Make sure you discuss the plan that is best for you with your estate-planning attorney. Getting your affairs in order is wise and lets you rest in confidence knowing that you have made provisions for your assets after you pass. If you haven't thought about estate planning, it is never too late or too early to start. Write the vision and make it plain. Seek out sound counsel and then execute a plan that will secure your wealth for years to come.

Write the vision and make it plain.

PLANNING YOUR RETIREMENT

And Abram was very rich in cattle, in silver,
and in gold.

—GENESIS 13:2

Riches and honour are with me; yea,
durable riches and righteousness.

—PROVERBS 8:18

Close your eyes for a moment and imagine yourself living on the beach sipping a tropical beverage as a cool breeze gently blows. You have no cares and no concerns. Your bank accounts are in the overflow, and you no longer have to punch a clock every morning. You are retired! This is a picture many people may have of themselves as they approach retirement. Vacation and travel are two things many retired people do, while others may choose to use their time differently. The one thing that should mark retirement, however, is the aspect of comfort. When you reach retirement, you should be in a position where you can live comfortably and do some of the things you really want to do. Retirement doesn't mean you are unproductive, it just means that your lifestyle can change from *having* to work every day to *choosing* how you want to spend your time. The key to experiencing relaxation during retirement is planning, and it is never too early to start that process.

The one thing that should mark retirement, however, is the aspect of comfort.

Before you get started with your retirement planning strategy, you want to ask yourself some key questions. You may want to start a journal specifically for the purpose of mapping out your plan and writing down questions, along with your answers. Gaining a concept of where you are now and what your vision for your retirement is will enable you to move forward with clarity and purpose.

1. What do you envision for your retirement? Does your ideal retirement life look like your current lifestyle? Identifying the quality of life you would like to experience when you retire is critical to shaping your savings goals.

2. What is your current salary? Your income is a good starting point for calculating your retirement savings needs. The more you make today, the more you will probably need in retirement because you will probably want to continue your current lifestyle into the retirement years. Be sure to take this into consideration when deciding how much to save.

3. How much will you collect from Social Security? Will you receive any defined pension benefits during retirement? These monthly payments can subtract substantially from the funds you have to save.

4. When will you retire? The younger you are at retirement, the longer you will probably live during retirement. Again, this means that you will need to save more. Waiting longer to retire means not only will you be retired for a shorter amount of time, obviously, but you will have also worked more years, which means you can save more.

5. How will you invest? The more aggressively you invest, the higher rate of return you can expect on your investments. This means you won't have to save as much, compared to the person who keeps his or her funds in a bank account that doesn't yield any return.

6. How much have you saved already, and how old are you now? The younger you are and the more you have saved, the less you'll have to save later to achieve the same quality of life as someone older or with less money saved up. Get a jump on the process by starting early.

Finding the Plan That's Right for You

You should familiarize yourself with the six different types of retirement plans as you prepare for your future. Let's take a look at them:

1. Individual Retirement Account (IRA)

An IRA is an investment account that allows you to contribute a certain amount of money each year and invest your contributions tax-deferred. What this means is that you are exempt from paying taxes on your annual investment gains. This enables your money to increase at a faster rate. When you withdraw the money upon retiring, you will pay income taxes on it. The money that is placed in an IRA can be invested in stocks, bonds, mutual funds, and other types of investments. You can buy and sell your investments within the IRA, but if you try to liquidate the funds prior to the designated retirement age of 59½, you are subject to a 10 percent penalty fee as well as local, state, and federal income taxes. Remember that your IRA is not supposed to be touched prior to retirement. You want to give your money the opportunity to grow over the years.

2. Roth IRA

The Roth IRA differs from a traditional IRA in that Roth contributions are made *after* taxes, but the money generated in the IRA is never taxed again afterwards. The benefit of this type of investment account is that you can withdraw funds prior to the retirement age without penalty fees. This is a great option if you want to grow your money and avoid future taxes on the investment.

3. 401(k) Account

A 401(k) is also known as a workplace retirement account. It is typically offered as an employee benefit through your job. With a 401(k), you contribute a portion of your pretax paycheck to a tax-deferred investment account. The benefit of a 401(k) account is that it lowers the amount of income your taxes are based on. Further, it allows your money to grow over time without being taxed. As with the IRA, however, you are penalized for withdrawing money from the account prior to retirement age. The 403(b) is a similar account for those who work for a nonprofit organization.

4. Roth 401(k)

A Roth 401(k) combines elements of the Roth IRA and the 401(k). Contributions come from your salary, post-taxes, and are never taxed again.

5. SIMPLE IRA

This retirement option is also known as a Savings Incentive Match for Employees IRA. It is a plan that small companies offer their employees that works very much like a 401(k). Contributions are made before taxes, and the money grows, tax-deferred, until retirement age.

6. SEP IRA

The SEP IRA is for those who are self-employed and have no employees. It allows you to contribute a portion of your income to your retirement fund and fully deduct it from your income taxes.

How Much to Save

When it comes to determining how much you should save for retirement, the idea is definitely the more, the better. Of course you want to save as much as possible early on so that you have a nice cushion to work with later. The closer you get to retirement, the more accurately you can see how close you are to your goals. Consider the following when determining your retirement savings plan:

The closer you get to retirement, the more accurately you can see how close you are to your goals.

1. Save at every available opportunity.

Initiating the process of saving for your retirement does not mean you have to begin with a large amount of money. Small savings add up over time, so starting small is better than not starting at all. Even if you can save twenty-five dollars a week, you will be heading in the right direction. Investing in tax-deferred accounts is the best way to see your money grow. Investment earnings are reinvested without tax penalties, which allow you to get more for your investment dollar. It's best to start saving early, so make sure you take part in any 401(k)/IRA accounts available through your employer.

2. Save at least as much as your employer will match.

If you are contributing to an employer-sponsored retirement plan such as a 401(k) or 403(b), find out if your employer offers matching contributions and increase the amount you contribute to get the full benefit of the employer match. A company will generally match up to 6 percent of an employee's income. Most plans "vest" over time, which means that the company will start by giving you 25 percent of the match and increase the percentage over the time that you are employed at the company. This means that after one or two years you may get 25 percent of your total vested amount; after three years you get 50 percent, four years get you 75 percent, and so on. When you are fully vested, you get 100 percent of your matching contributions.

3. Save at least 10 percent of your gross income.

Ten percent of your gross income is a great target goal for those who want to save for retirement. Set up automatic deposits from your checking account so you don't even have to think about setting the money aside each month.

4. Save raises and bonuses instead of spending them.

One of the biggest financial mistakes people make is spending additional money that comes into the household rather than saving it. The temptation to spend all excess is great, especially with so many things that we would like to purchase to give us a sense of immediate gratification. It is important to renew your mind, however, and think about your future rather than sacrifice your financial future for the sake of today's enjoyment. Whenever additional money comes into your hands, whether a raise or a bonus, look at it as an opportunity to invest in your future. Settle it beforehand that you will put any additional money aside for your retirement savings. If you have already set up automatic deposits, you probably don't even notice the money missing from your regular paycheck. When you have become disciplined in this, the next objective is to automatically stash away extra income that you don't immediately need. If you know that you will be receiving a raise, set up an automatic deposit into your savings account in advance.

5. As you get closer to retirement, continue to save more.

Even if you didn't start saving for your retirement until later on in life, you can still take advantage of the government's provisions to help you catch up. If you are fifty years or older, you can add $5,500 more to your tax-deferred retirement account under a provision called "catch up contributions." If you are in this age group, take advantage of this option as soon as possible.

6. Save after-tax cash.

If you have capitalized on all the tax-favored options that are available through your employer and you have cash to spare, that money can be funneled into a savings account. It is best to put it in a Roth IRA, as the money is invested *after* taxes. This enables the money in your Roth to grow tax-free. Roth IRA funds can also be withdrawn before you retire without penalty.

Before You Retire

As with anything else that requires planning, you will want to assess some things before you retire. First, you need to evaluate your assets. Assets are things you own. To calculate your assets, start with your retirement accounts. Make a checklist with these questions to determine the total of all your accounts:

- How much do I have in my regular IRA?
- What is the value of my Roth IRA?
- Did I contribute to an employer retirement plan such as a 401(k) or 403(b)?
- Do I have a SEP IRA or SIMPLE IRA?
- Do I own any annuities or whole life insurance policies?
- How much do I have in my savings account?
- How much do I have in my checking account?

- What is the value of my investment accounts, including taxable brokerage accounts, mutual funds, stocks, bonds, or CDs?

When looking at your assets, don't forget to factor in your home, car(s), and other personal property such as rental property. The total value of everything (including your retirement and nonretirement accounts) equals your assets.

Next, you want to evaluate your debts. This is important because sometimes the debt factor can cause your retirement plan to change. You want to look at things like the mortgage on your home, your home equity loan, car loans or leases, consumer debt from retail stores, any outstanding medical bills, student loans, etc. If your debts exceed your assets, realistically you won't be able to retire right away. If you are practically debt-free, you have more leeway. If you have significant debt, you will want to come up with a plan to pay it off as quickly as possible because who and what you are will impact the quality of your life when you retire. Any funds you are using to make payments on high-interest credit cards will take away from what you could have at your disposal when you retire. Your monthly debt obligation is an important component to consider when evaluating your retirement income and expenses.

Retirement planning has changed over the years because of demographic and lifestyle changes. For example, life expectancies are rising and early retirements are more frequent, often because of health concerns and layoffs. When you take these things into consideration, it means that the working career of most people will generally be shorter and you will need to sustain yourself for many more years in retirement than those in previous generations. Here are a few things to keep in mind:

*Retirement planning has changed over the years
because of demographic and lifestyle changes.*

• Take advantage of the defined benefit pension plan. Your pension is often calculated based on the extra hours you work during your last years on your job prior to retiring, or any additional years you worked (length of service).

• Manage your Social Security benefits. Most people qualify for Social Security, which is also a defined benefit pension plan. What is interesting to note is that Social Security is indexed for inflation, which means your monthly payment rises over the years that you are in retirement. Be sure to understand how early retirement can affect your benefits and evaluate whether you can avoid taking your benefits before the normal retirement age and receiving the permanent benefit reduction that comes as a result.

• Save as much as intelligently possible to set yourself up for a comfortable life should you retire early. Take full advantage of employee benefit plans such as IRAs, 401(k)s, and 403(b)s.

• Max out your Roth IRA. The tax-free nature of this investment account makes it a powerful tool to help you get the most out of your retirement years.

Saving for retirement is an aspect of being a good steward over your finances and will put you in a position to enjoy the fruits of your labor, whether you retire early or later in life (Ecclesiastes

5:18–19). With so many vehicles to help move you into a prosperous lifestyle in your retirement years, there is no reason why you cannot set yourself up for a quality of life that is rewarding and enjoyable. Start today and own your future through discipline and diligent financial planning.

Start today and own your future through discipline and diligent financial planning.

LIFE INSURANCE: PREPARE FOR YOUR FUTURE

The blessing of the Lord, it maketh rich, and he addeth no sorrow with it.

—PROVERBS 10:22

For he hath strengthened the bars of thy gates; he hath blessed thy children within thee.

—PSALM 147:13

Let's face it: Especially when we are in the prime of life, none of us want to think about the practical details that need to be taken care of when we die. Funeral costs, burial expenses, and asset disbursement are not the most pleasant things to have to plan for; however, death is a part of life. And many things have to be done when that time comes. Because end-of-life details are difficult to think about, some people don't give them much thought at all, which unfortunately complicates things when they pass away. Part of being a good steward over our wealth and resources involves utilizing the practical tools available to us to plan, effectively and efficiently, for inevitable events such as death. Life insurance is something you definitely want to incorporate as part of your planning process.

If you were to die today, would your family be able to handle the situation financially? Not only is a loved one's passing emotionally devastating and draining, but the post-death expenses can be overwhelming. Funeral costs, for example, can easily exceed twenty thousand dollars when you are looking at caskets, burial sites, and morticians' fees. And if lingering medical expenses must be paid after death, the financial burden can quickly reach a breaking point. When you don't have life insurance, someone will be left to foot the bill. And if family members do not have the money to cover these costs, it will be a very bad situation.

This is why it is important to make the necessary provisions by purchasing life insurance, which will cover funeral costs and even help contribute to your family's living expenses after you pass. Making sure that your own funeral costs are covered and that your family members do not have to carry the burden of all the postmortem expenses is one of the most caring things you can do for them.

If you were to die today, would your family be able to handle the situation financially?

In essence, life insurance is something that is there whenever you need it. You can structure a policy any way you want it so that family members can focus on their grieving process without the additional burden of financial responsibilities. So many different types of life insurance exist, which can be confusing and overwhelming, but the thing to keep in mind when looking at different options is that if you don't need a certain option, don't buy it. Focus on what you need and go from there.

Life insurance needs vary depending on your personal situation. You definitely want to get life insurance if you have dependents, or a spouse. You especially need to get life insurance if you are the primary breadwinner in the household or contribute significantly to the household income. You want to make sure that recurring bills and obligations such as mortgage payments and any revolving debts are covered if you die. You should take into consideration all the factors in the situation when deciding what type of life insurance to purchase.

Life insurance needs vary depending on your personal situation.

Types of Life Insurance

Several different types of life insurance are available to you. Whole, term, universal, variable, and variable-universal are all options. A debate has always existed about whether term life insurance is a better option than whole life insurance. Some financial experts recommend that if you are under forty years old and don't have a family disposition for a life-threatening illness, then term insurance is your best option. Term insurance offers a death benefit but has no cash value. Whole life insurance offers both a death benefit and cash value, but it is much more expensive. These are just some of the things you will need to consider when deciding what policy is best for you. Let's take a look at the different types of life insurance and the pros and cons of each:

1. Whole Life Insurance

Whole life insurance is basically permanent life insurance protection for your entire life, usually to age one hundred. A whole life policy is contractually guaranteed not to lapse, as long as you pay sufficient premiums each year to keep the policy in force. Besides permanent lifetime insurance protection, whole life insurance features a savings element that allows you to build cash value on a tax-deferred basis. A portion of the premiums you pay build up the savings aspect of the policy and are invested by the company. The interest rate return on your investment is added to the savings portion of the policy. This is how the policy builds cash value.

The pros of whole life insurance are the cash value/savings aspect and the fact that the money is tax-deferred. If the contract is set up properly in advance, you might build up enough cash value to stop paying premiums by a certain age, or to be able to borrow from the cash value (take a policy loan) during your lifetime on a tax-advantaged basis. While term life insurance premiums eventually rise after the initial guarantee period, whole life insurance premiums will not increase during your lifetime (as long as you pay the planned amount and repay any policy loans).

On the flip side, whole life insurance has some cons. For example, you are not allowed to choose separate investment accounts such as money market, stocks, or bonds. The insurance company controls how and where your premium dollars are invested. Whole life insurance offers no premium flexibility either; the plan you buy today remains fixed for life. It is therefore important to plan carefully, because whole life insurance is not adaptable.

2. Variable Life Insurance

Variable life insurance is also known as *variable appreciable life insurance*. It provides a permanent benefit protection to your beneficiary upon your death. This type of life insurance is "variable" because it allows you to designate a portion of your premium dollars to a separate account made up of various investment funds within the insurance company's portfolio, such as an equity fund, a money market fund, a bond fund, or some combination thereof. Because it is variable, the value of the death benefit and the cash value may fluctuate, depending on the performance of the investment portion of the policy. Although most variable life insurance policies guarantee that the death benefit will not fall below a specified minimum, a minimum cash value is seldom guaranteed. Variable is a form of whole life insurance, and because of investment risks, it is also considered a securities contract (a guarantee of a settlement).

Variable life insurance allows you to participate in different types of investments like mutual funds, stocks, bonds, etc., while not being taxed on your earnings (until you surrender the policy). You can apply interest earned on these investments toward the premiums, which can potentially lower your payment amounts.

Unfortunately, because this type of insurance involves investing your money in things like mutual funds and stocks, the risk exists that when those investment vehicles perform poorly, you can lose money. This can translate into your having to pay more than you can afford to keep the policy in effect. It also means that the cash and/or death benefit of the insurance policy may decline. Another aspect of variable life insurance is that you are not able to withdraw money from the total cash value while you are alive.

3. Universal Life Insurance

Universal life insurance (UL), also called *flexible premium adjustable life insurance*, is a more flexible version of whole life insurance. Like whole life, universal life insurance offers a savings element that grows on a tax-deferred basis. The insurance company invests a portion of your premiums in bonds, mortgages, and money market funds. The return on the investments is credited to your policy, tax-deferred. A guaranteed minimum interest rate applied to the policy (usually around 4 percent) means that the insurance company guarantees a certain minimum return on your money, regardless of how the investments perform. If the insurance company does well with its investments, the interest rate return on the accumulated cash value will increase.

Universal life also offers two death benefit options. The first pays the death benefit out of the policy's cash value. The more cash value that has accumulated means the less the company has to pay out. The second option pays the face amount stated in the contract plus any cash values that have accumulated over the years. Many universal life insurance policies today offer a no-lapse guarantee: As long as you pay the minimum designated premium, the policy will stay in effect to age one hundred (or even to age 120). Paying the minimum guaranteed premium, however, is rarely sufficient to build up significant cash values.

One of the unique aspects of universal life is that it doesn't have the strict rules associated with traditional whole life insurance, which requires policy owners to pay their premiums before the end of the grace period, or the policy lapses. Universal life insurance policy owners can pay the exact amount of the billed premium, more than the billed premium, or less than the billed premium, and they can pay when they desire. They can even choose to pay no premium at all. Universal life insurance represents a significant change from traditional fixed premium whole life insurance products.

Despite the premium flexibility of universal life insurance, certain rules apply to premium payments. Although a policyholder may choose not to pay a premium on a particular premium due date, any payments that he makes must meet a certain minimum to help the carrier manage the costs of premium collection and processing. Typically three premiums are associated with universal life insurance policies:

1. Minimum premiums

2. Target premiums

3. Maximum premiums

The minimum premium is the premium that, if paid each year, would generally be just enough to keep the policy in effect for one more year without the accumulation of any cash value. The universal life insurance target premium is the amount of premium that will keep the policy in force for the insured's lifetime. There is, however, no guarantee that the universal life insurance policy will remain in force for that period if only the target premium is paid. In fact, there is no guarantee that the universal life insurance policy will remain in force regardless of the premium level that the policy owner maintains.

The maximum premium is the largest permitted premium that will enable the universal life insurance policy to maintain its status as life insurance. If you pay additional premiums, the policy will be considered a Modified Endowment Contract or MEC. MECs lose many of the tax advantages of life insurance.

The pros of universal life insurance are obviously that it gives you the flexibility to adjust the death benefit as your needs change, as well as the flexibility to pay smaller or larger premiums—depending on your financial situation. This is often an important feature for families who may have fluctuations in their ability to pay.

The cons are that if your premium payments are too small for too long, the policy could lapse, leaving you without insurance protection. Also, if the insurance company does poorly with its investments, the interest return on the cash portion of the policy will decrease.

How Do I Know If I Need Life Insurance Right Now?

Keep in mind that your need for life insurance depends on your personal situation right now. Not everyone needs to go out and buy a policy. You need to consider the purpose and also take into consideration certain things such as whether you are single, married, or have dependents. If people are relying on the income that you are bringing in, then life insurance is something to consider. If, however, you have no dependents, there really is no need to purchase it. At the same time, if you are planning to have a family in the future, you may consider a term policy, which enables you to secure lower costs, especially if you buy it when you are young.

Keep in mind that your need for life insurance depends on your personal situation right now.

Again, whether you need life insurance and the amount that you need depend on whether you have other sources of income, if you have dependents or debts, and your lifestyle in general. Typically you will want to purchase a policy that is between five and ten times your annual salary. To calculate your need, make a list of your household's annual expenses, which would include your mortgage payment, things like day-care expenses, monthly debt payments, and education costs. Multiply the total by the number of years you need the insurance to cover. Be sure to add in funeral and burial costs as well.

Life insurance costs are based on what are called *actuarial tables*, which are used to project a person's life expectancy. People who are high-risk include those with preexisting health conditions, those who are overweight or smoke, and those who engage in dangerous hobbies, occupations, or sports. These people will pay higher rates than a low-risk policyholder.

Financial advisors recommend keeping your life insurance and your investments separate. The line of thought here is that if you need life insurance, you should buy term life insurance, which is set for a specific term such as ten to thirty years, and has a much lower premium than whole life. If you want to invest in stocks, bonds, and mutual funds, do it yourself.

As with any monetary decision, you may want to consider consulting a financial advisor who can give you sound, objective counsel where life insurance is concerned. Know your options, seek God, and determine what is best for you and your family. Life insurance is a great way to secure financial stability for your loved ones for when you pass, and it is something to consider if you know you will leave significant financial responsibilities that they will not be able to handle on their own. This is another way to exercise good stewardship over the resources God blesses you with.

Know your options, seek God, and determine what is best for you and your family.

LOANS: BORROWING AND BUILDING FOR YOUR FUTURE

10

The blessing of the Lord, it maketh rich, and he addeth no sorrow with it.

—PROVERBS 10:22

But my God shall supply all your need according to his riches in glory by Christ Jesus.

—PHILIPPIANS 4:19

You may have heard that borrowing money is an absolute no-no. Perhaps you have seen friends or family members get into financial difficulty because they borrowed money that they could not repay. Maybe you have even gotten into a financial bind because of unwise decisions in the past. While it is true that borrowing money should not be a way of life for a Christian, sometimes it is necessary to obtain a loan for certain purposes. The key is to understand how the loan system works and how to make it work to your advantage. I often say that when you don't understand the purpose for something, abuse is inevitable. When you understand how to use loans properly, and the importance of evaluating what it will take for you to pay them back in a timely manner, they can be a benefit to you.

While it is true that borrowing money should not be a way of life for a Christian, sometimes it is necessary to obtain a loan for certain purposes.

Many reasons exist for getting a loan. Most people do not have huge lump sums of money on hand to purchase items they need, such as a home, car, or education. Even starting your own business requires significant funds that you need to be readily available. Loans allow you to take advantage of opportunities that your current income does not afford. What you do with the money you obtain from a loan can actually help you build a better future for yourself and your family, if you are wise. The key term here is *wisdom*.

A loan can be an investment into your future rather than a liability, *if* you calculate the cost. For example, if borrowing money for an education increases your potential to earn more money in the future, it is a good investment. The same is true with getting a loan for a business idea God has given you or borrowing money in order to purchase a home, which is one of the best decisions you can make. A home builds equity, which gives you financial freedom later on. Being smart with loans can even help build or improve your credit when you pay them back on time, which increases your chances of being approved for more loans in the future. To sum it up, loans provide you with access to growth, the pursuit of opportunities, and success.

Just as some debt can work for you and help put you ahead, some debt you should most definitely avoid. Consumer debt is the type most people rack up, and it ends up putting them in a financial bind. When you think of consumer debt, think of credit cards. Again, if the purpose of a thing is not understood, it will be abused. This is usually the case when it comes to how people use credit cards.

We live in a world that is driven by a "microwave mentality." This is the mind-set that drives hyperconsumption, which is consistently buying things you can't afford simply to possess them. Credit card companies and retailers thrive on the lack of self-control that today's consumer exhibits. Shopping malls and sales representatives use strategies to draw people in and make them feel they *have* to have what they are selling right away. Because many people are not disciplined where their finances are concerned, they fall right into the sales traps laid for them at their favorite department stores. A credit card seems like a quick solution to getting what you want when you don't have the cash, but the consequences of unwisely using credit cards can be tremendously damaging to your life. Not only can you accumulate high amounts of debt in a short period of time that you cannot immediately pay off, but you end up paying *more* for the items you bought because of interest rates and credit card fees. This is not the way God wants us to operate.

> *We live in a world that is driven by a "microwave mentality."*

Being a good steward over your money is an important key to God's releasing more money into your hands. You can never get to the point of walking in true wealth and riches if you don't master the finances you currently have. Using credit cards unwisely puts you in a position of having to use money that could be invested elsewhere to make monthly payments for items that you could have paid cash for had you exercised patience and waited. Credit cards should not be used this way. A great rule of thumb when it comes to buying things on credit is: If you can't pay the balance off by the end of the month, don't make the purchase. Credit cards should be used only for emergencies *or* if you are absolutely certain that you can pay the balance off within the billing cycle. If you can't do this, simply don't use credit cards.

> *If you can't pay the balance off by the end of the month, don't make the purchase.*

Who Are the Lenders?

Institutions that lend money are varied, and you have to locate the option that is best for you, as different ones offer loans for a range of purposes. A great place to start investigating loan options is your own bank. Keep in mind that the bank is not the only entity that offers loans. You may also consider:

- Credit Unions

Credit unions are banks whose members are also its joint owners. Decisions about interest rates and other policies are made by a voting board of bank members, which results in policies that are designed to benefit those members.

- Credit-Only Banks

Some financial institutions have the FDIC-protected status of banks, but they offer only credit lines and other loan products. These institutions are where you will find a wider variety of loans that cover homes and businesses.

- Home Financiers/Mortgagors

Some companies exclusively deal with home loans and financing. These are great for those who are new to the home-buying process because they walk clients through the process of obtaining a home loan in a step-by-step fashion.

- New and Used Vehicle Dealers

Many automobile dealerships offer loans to customers on-site. Be sure to explore all your options before making a final decision on who will finance your car loan. You may discover something better by shopping around.

- Payday Lenders

These lenders' primary focus is to advance customers a portion of their next paycheck. There are fees associated with these loans, which doesn't make them the best choice. You don't want to become trapped in the cycle of getting cash advances on a consistent basis through a lender.

- Educational Lenders

Some financial institutions specifically deal with student loans, including the federally backed Stafford loans and PLUS loans. Interest rates typically remain the same across the board, but some banks offer the option to consolidate once you have entered your repayment period. Remember that an educational loan is an investment in your future because it helps you pursue a career that will benefit you financially in the long run.

How to Apply for a Loan

If you've never applied for a loan, don't worry; it is not a difficult process. The first step is to decide exactly how much you want to borrow. Lean more toward the conservative side and explore other options to assist you in fulfilling your dream, such as borrowing money from a family member or tapping into your personal savings account to help finance your goal. The objective is to avoid extremely large amounts of debt as much as possible. Remember that wisdom is the most important thing here. When you have a good idea of how much money you will need to borrow, seek out a lender that specializes in that amount of money. The loan conversation is always going to start with how much you need, which will then give the lender an idea of whether that amount is something it is comfortable forwarding to you.

References are important when looking for a lender. Never underestimate the power and importance of relationships. If you can find a reputable lender that family members or friends have had good experiences with, it will ease your mind. The relationship between the borrower and the lender needs to be a positive one fostered by open communication and trust. Bringing someone on board who has already worked with someone you know is a smart idea.

References are important when looking for a lender.

The next step after choosing a lender is the loan application. This is the part that can be tedious because typically you must fill out and submit a lot of paperwork. The information on the loan application focuses on two primary things: your income and your credit. The lender will need copies of your tax returns and/or pay stubs, and it will run a credit check on you from at least one of the major credit reporting agencies. Because of this, you will want to be familiar with your credit report prior to applying for the loan. Generally, it is a good idea to be abreast of your personal credit score anyway so that you know where you stand. Pull your report every year to keep tabs on it.

Whether we want to accept it or not, our credit report is basically a picture of our financial character, and it can be the determining factor in whether we are able to gain access to certain resources or not. This is why it is so important to make financial decisions that will protect your credit. When you are going through the loan application process, you may need to explain discrepancies on your report, or expound on why certain things are there. If you have made some bad financial decisions that are reflected on your report, explain them to the lender and be sure to include what you have done or are currently doing to correct the issue. Transparency and a clearly articulated plan of action can work in your favor, even if your credit report is less than stellar.

Once you have submitted your application, the only thing left to do is to wait for approval. Sometimes the lender will need more documentation or other information to complete the process. The lender should let you know when you can expect to hear back regarding its decision. If it does not approve you for a loan, don't give up; many lenders may be willing to work with you. One closed door does not mean another will not open. Sometimes you may even need to rework the terms of the loan or apply for a lower amount. There are many ways to achieve your goal when it comes to borrowing money, so do not become discouraged.

One closed door does not mean another will not open.

Lenders look for some key things when considering approving a loan for a borrower. They are taking a risk and want to make sure that the decision to loan you money will not end up costing them in the end. For example, when a loan is secured against a purchase, such as a mortgage for a home, there is always the risk of foreclosure, which means they will have to find another buyer in order to recoup the loss. If the loan is unsecured, they risk losing the *entire* amount of the loan or having to go through collections, which is a hassle and does not guarantee recovery of the funds.

These risks are why lenders are very meticulous when it comes to covering all their bases and making sure that the borrower is not a liability. The most important thing a lender is looking for is whether the borrower has a high probability of paying back the loan. This is why credit history, current income, and the amount of debt you currently have are major factors. Even if you have debt, it is a good sign to a lender when you have a history of making timely payments to your creditors, as well as keeping your credit card balances to a minimum rather than maxing them out. High balances on credit cards are a major red flag to a lender. They want to see that you are financially prepared to repay the loan in a consistent, timely manner and that you have not overextended yourself with debts you cannot repay or that they perceive will interfere with the repayment of the loan you are applying for.

Counting the Cost of Borrowing Money

As I mentioned before, borrowing money can actually be a tool you can use to get ahead in life. As with any financial decision that has the potential to impact your future, however, it is critical to count the cost of getting a loan. When you receive a loan, you pay for the privilege of having funds extended to you that you would not normally have access to. Nothing is free! The cost of a loan comes in two forms:

Borrowing money can actually be a tool you can use to get ahead in life.

1. Interest

Interest is a percentage of the original loan amount (also known as the *principal*) that the lender charges over time until the loan is repaid. Generally, interest is charged on the total outstanding balance. For example, if you have a loan for $100 at 5 percent interest, then your total loan after one year, if you make no payments, is $105. If after two years, the loan amount grows to $110.25, this is what is known as *compound interest*. Compound interest adds considerably to the total cost of a loan over time. Many loans have both interest and fees, which make the loan more costly.

Lenders are typically willing to extend loans to borrowers based on the profit they make in interest and fees. In the case of student loans, the government regulates this profit margin, and in other situations interest rates are set as high as the lender feels it can get without being undercut by its competition. Remember that the loan business is just that—a business. Whether interest rates are government regulated or not, they are usually set relative to standard markers that apply to the entire industry.

You will want to lock-in your interest rate if possible. To lock-in your rate means that you get a guarantee from your lender that your interest rate will not go up for a designated time period. It may be for the entire life of the loan or a smaller period of time. Particularly as it relates to home loans, you really want to try to lock-in a rate. This is the best way to ensure that there are no unexpected changes to your monthly payments.

Sometimes lenders offer lower variable interest rates as a way to bait borrowers, only to have the interest rate go up later on. If you know that you will be able to accommodate changes in your interest rate, then a variable rate will not be a huge issue for you. Still, the wiser decision is to pay a slightly higher interest rate and get it locked-in so that your payments remain stable over time.

2. Fees

Loan fees are generally unregulated. At the end of the day, you have to decide whether or not the convenience of having a loan extended to you is worth the fees you may have to pay.

Understanding the Terms of the Loan

I cannot emphasize enough how important it is: If you are going to be a borrower, you must be ready to pay. Getting a loan is not an agreement you should enter into haphazardly but something that you should carefully consider. There is an agreement included in the loan that requires you to repay the loan within a certain amount of time. It is absolutely your responsibility to meet the terms of this agreement and hold up your end.

If you cannot repay your loan, the lender can and will take action against you. Foreclosure, collections agencies, a negative report to the credit agencies, and wage garnishments are all things you want to avoid at all costs. This is why it is essential that you do not take out a loan that you do not foresee yourself being able to repay. Taking out a loan simply because you need quick cash is not a good decision. If you are going to borrow money, honestly evaluate your monthly income and expenses as well as your budget. Just because you can get a loan doesn't mean you are in a position to repay it.

Just because you can get a loan doesn't mean you are in a position to repay it.

Many times people get loans that they cannot pay, and they end up going into default status. Defaulting on a loan is very serious. What it means is that if a certain number of payments have not been made, the lender will put the loan in "default" and begin the repossession process, or get a collection agency involved. When you are not proactive in bringing a loan out of default status, it will affect your credit rating and potentially cause serious financial problems. Lenders are not lenient when it comes to recouping the money they have advanced to you. When a loan is in default, you can expect constant phone calls, correspondence via mail, and even wage garnishment if you continue to ignore the lender, particularly if it is a student loan or other government-issued loan. Do everything you can to get your loan out of default by paying the amount of missed payments as expeditiously as possible. There may even be payment plans available to do this. The key is to communicate with the lenders and not avoid them.

Fortunately, there are options such as deferment and forbearance, which enable you to defer your payments for a certain amount of time if you can provide information that states you are having financial difficulties and cannot meet the terms of your loan agreement. Just remember that these options do not release you from the debt but rather give you a little space to get your finances together without penalty. You will still be expected to begin making payments once the deferment period is over.

Research and investigation are the keys to making sound decisions where loans are concerned. You shouldn't look at them as a bad decision, but as something to help you get ahead in life. Of course, if you do not have to get a loan because you have the cash available to do whatever you are trying to do, by all means use cash. But if you find that a loan is the only option for you to accomplish your goal at the time, and you have carefully counted the cost, prayed, and gotten clearance from the Holy Spirit on the matter, you can move forward in confidence. When you allow a loan to be a means to an end and don't overextend yourself, it can position you to reach your wealthy place.

*Research and investigation are the keys
to making sound decisions where
loans are concerned.*

11

THE POWER OF GOOD CREDIT

A gracious woman retaineth honour: and strong
men retain riches.

—PROVERBS 11:16

But thou shalt remember the Lord thy God: for it
is he that giveth thee power to get wealth, that he
may establish his covenant which he sware unto
thy fathers, as it is this day.

—DEUTERONOMY 8:18

Did you know that your financial character is judged by how good (or bad) your credit is? Well, at least in the world it is. Credit is one of the markers that financial institutions and even employers look at when considering you for loans and employment. Most of us are not taught about the importance of maintaining good credit and, as a result, we make bad financial decisions that cost us later on in life. This is not to say that credit cannot be repaired, but how much farther would we be on the path to wealth if we had learned about the importance of maintaining good credit earlier in life? No matter where you are financially right now, it is never too late to turn things around. Understanding the power of good credit is essential to your having access to resources and opportunities that can position you for prosperity.

No matter where you are financially right now,
it is never too late to turn things around.

There are many definitions of credit, but what really sums it up is *financial trustworthiness*. Your credit history may be the most important factor that lenders look at when you apply for a loan. This means that our ability to acquire a car, a home, or a credit card or start a business with borrowed money depends on our credit. It quickly becomes obvious why this is such an important aspect of our financial profiles. The better our credit, the more options we will have. Lenders are more willing to work with individuals with good credit, as well as offer them better terms and lower interest rates. Building a good credit history is essential to achieving financial independence and ultimately walking in the level of financial prosperity that God designed for our lives. We must not only do the spiritual part of things, but we also have to operate within the guidelines and rules that have been established in this world so that we can capitalize on the resources available to us. Credit is an essential part of this.

How to Build Good Credit

Credit cards are one of the most misused financial tools available today. Most people had to learn the hard way, through trial and error, about building their credit, particularly as it relates to credit cards. Many of us were, at one time, irresponsible college students who abused credit cards that we received in the mail. Thousands of dollars later, we realized that those past decisions would come back to haunt us in the form of collections agencies that had no problem harassing us with endless phone calls! Credit card companies target young, naïve students who are eager to spend money they don't have by charging to a credit card. It seems harmless at first, but when those balances become unmanageable, we realize we have made some serious mistakes.

Credit cards can be a benefit or a nightmare. On one hand, they can serve as a credit-building tool if we use them responsibly. On the other hand, they can become a source of financial bondage when we abuse them. I encourage people to be mindful about accepting many of the "free" credit card offers that come in the mail. Most of those cards end up having extremely high interest rates and annual fees. Research different cards before accepting any offer, and consider getting a credit card through your bank that is connected to your checking account. These cards usually offer overdraft protection on your account, which is an added benefit. You always want to take into consideration the annual percentage rate and any other fees that are associated with the card before submitting the application.

Credit cards can be a benefit or a nightmare.

Unfortunately, people use credit cards to fulfill their desire for immediate gratification. Department store administrators know this, which is why they try to lure you into opening a high-interest credit card account. They offer customers a small discount on their purchases if they take out a line of credit during a purchase. They know that consumers will be more likely to continue spending money in their store if they can whip out a credit card rather than use cash. This is because credit cards present the illusion of being able to buy whatever you want, whenever you want, without penalty. For the person who has an issue with hyperconsumption, credit cards are extremely dangerous. I would encourage people to stay away from retail credit cards at all costs because they are a financial trap that will end up costing you in the long run.

The penalty for abusing credit cards is greater than the card owner ever imagined. An item that was initially priced at fifty dollars ends up costing one hundred dollars over a period of six months, once interest and other fees are factored into the equation. The tendency to overspend on items that you want immediately is greater when you have credit cards, which is why you have to understand the purpose of the card before getting one.

Despite the negative consequences of credit card abuse, using credit cards the right way can help your credit tremendously, but it takes discipline. The key is to remember that if you cannot pay off your credit card balance by the billing cycle, or if it is not an emergency, you don't need to use the card. A good idea would be to find a card that offers a small line of credit so that you can keep your balance low. For someone just starting out with credit cards, I would not get a card with a credit line higher than $250. Another option is to get a secured credit card, which simply means that you "load" the credit card with money yourself. This enables you to control your spending more effectively. Rather than accepting a credit card with a $5,000 credit line, choose one that will give you no option other than to keep a very low balance. This way you will not be able to run up a bill you cannot afford to pay, while simultaneously establishing good credit history. Be sure to pay your credit card bill on time and pay more than the minimum payment. Keeping extremely low balances on your card(s) also looks good on your credit report. The more lines of credit you have open and the more of them that are bordering the credit limit, the more derogatory marks you will receive on your credit report.

Be sure to pay your credit card bill on time and pay more than the minimum payment.

There are other ways to help build and maintain good credit, such as paying your bills on time (non-credit-card-related bills), making more than the minimum payments on your credit cards, and not applying for a lot of credit in a short period of time. The more credit inquiries you have from lending companies on your report, the more negative it looks. You want to have some credit accounts open, but not an abundance of them. This demonstrates that you do not recklessly open credit card accounts and run up the balances with no way to pay them off. Conservative spending and timely payments are the keys to good credit.

Conservative spending and timely payments
are the keys to good credit.

Understanding Your Credit Report

Your credit report is a record of your borrowing and repaying habits. It records any credit card accounts and loans you may have, as well as the balances and how regularly you make the payments. Every missed payment and past-due balance is recorded on your credit report, along with any defaulted loans. It also shows if any company has taken action against you as a result of outstanding balances that you have not paid.

Your credit information is gathered and recorded by what is called a consumer reporting agency (CRA). Three primary agencies collect information about your credit activity, house it in a database, and then charge a fee to provide you with the information in the credit report. The three credit bureaus are Equifax, TransUnion, and Experian.

The information on your credit report, which outlines your borrowing, charging, and repayment activities, determines your credit score. A good credit score positions you for financial success while a poor score can hinder you from reaching your goals. The credit score is essentially a mathematical score that weighs elements of your credit report to predict your level of future risk. Lenders will use their own scoring systems to evaluate and project customer risk.

As I stated earlier, your credit report and score can play a role in whether you are able to buy a home or even get a certain job, which is why it is so important to make good financial decisions to protect your credit at all costs. Pay your bills on time and don't take on debt that you cannot pay back in a timely manner.

Credit bureaus can provide information to five primary places:

1. Creditors or lenders that are considering granting or have granted you credit or a loan.

2. Employers considering you for employment, promotion, reassignment, or retention.

3. Insurers considering you for an insurance policy or reviewing an existing policy.

4. Government agencies reviewing your financial status or government benefits.

5. Anyone else with a legitimate business need for the information, such as a potential landlord with whom you are entering into a lease agreement.

There are typically four types of information on a credit report that you should be aware of:

1. *Identifying Information*: Your full name, any known aliases, current and previous addresses, Social Security number, year of birth, current and past employers, and, if applicable, similar information about your spouse.

2. *Credit Information*: The accounts you have with banks, retailers, credit card issuers, utility companies, and other lenders (accounts are listed by type of loan, such as mortgage, student

loan, revolving credit, or installment loan; the date you opened the account; your credit limit or the loan amount; any cosigners on the loan; and your payment pattern over the past two years).

3. *Public Record Information*: State and county court records on bankruptcy, tax liens, or monetary judgments (some consumer reporting agencies list nonmonetary judgments as well).

4. *Recent Inquiries*: The names of those who have obtained copies of your credit report within the past year (two years for employment purposes).

Credit bureaus collect information from parties that have previously extended credit to you, such as a department store that issued you a credit card or a bank that granted you a personal loan. The lenders themselves make the decision about whether or not to grant you credit. The credit reporting companies only supply the information about your credit history.

It is so important to obtain a copy of your credit report every year in order to stay informed about your situation and to avoid any unwelcome surprises, particularly before you apply for any loans, mortgages, or credit cards. Keep in mind that credit reporting discrepancies are not uncommon and can be rectified if you take action. If you notice something on your credit report that is suspicious or inaccurate, such as a misspelled name, wrong address, or credit accounts that you did not open, you should contact the credit reporting agency immediately and dispute the item. The company is then responsible for researching and changing or removing incorrect data. This process may take up to forty-five days, but it is in your best interest because you do not want anything derogatory on your report. At your request, a corrected report will be sent to those parties that you specify, who have received your report within the past six months, or employers who have received it within the last two years.

You are probably wondering how long your credit history remains on your credit report. Regardless of whether your history is good or bad, all your credit information stays on your report for seven years. Personal bankruptcies remain on your credit report for ten years.

It is easy to obtain a copy of your credit report from any of the three credit reporting agencies, and you are entitled to receive one free credit report every twelve months from each of them. This free credit file can be requested through www.annualcreditreport. com or by contacting the companies directly by phone or mail. To process your request, you will need to provide your name, current and previous addresses, Social Security number, and date of birth. Also, to verify your identity, other information such as a copy of your driver's license, utility bill(s), or a bank statement may be required. Keep in mind that the content of your credit report, including your credit score, can be different at each bureau, so it's a good idea to request copies from each one. To contact the three major credit bureaus write, call, or visit their Web sites at:

Equifax
PO Box 105873
Atlanta, GA 30348
http://www.equifax.com
(800) 685-1111

Experian (formerly TRW)
PO Box 2104
Allen, TX 75013-2104
http://www.experian.com
(888) 397-3742

TransUnion
Consumer Disclosure Center
PO Box 1000
Chester, PA 19022
http://www.transunion.com
(800) 916-8800 or (800) 888-4213

Staying on top of your credit report and being aware of your score is going to help keep you focused on remaining disciplined with your financial habits. It will also give you a clear picture of how your past financial decisions have affected your credit score. God always entrusts us with more when we have demonstrated that we are good stewards over what we currently have. Having credit extended to you is a privilege that is contingent upon your integrity and character, so be wise. How we deal with the resources available to us in the natural realm shows how well we will handle more and greater financial *and* spiritual responsibilities.

> *God always entrusts us with more when we have demonstrated that we are good stewards over what we currently have.*

If you have made some financial mistakes that have set you back, do not get discouraged. Starting today, you can turn the tide by making wiser choices, such as paying your bills on time, living within your means, and refusing to use credit for immediate gratification purposes.

If you have overwhelming credit card debt that you cannot pay back right now, consider consulting a credit counseling service that can help you consolidate your debt. When you go through this type of program, your credit cards are deactivated so you can no longer use them. In addition, this type of credit counseling service can help you get your debt under control, challenge any discrepancies on your report, and follow up with the credit reporting agencies. Instead of running from your creditors, write them letters explaining your situation and petition them to work out a payment arrangement with you. Most creditors are willing to work with clients who demonstrate that they have full intentions of paying off their debt. Change starts the moment you decide to take a different path. The choice is yours. God's supernatural power and favor will get involved with your situation when you release your faith and apply corresponding action by taking the necessary steps to position yourself for financial increase.

Change starts the moment you decide to take a different path.

12

HANDLING YOUR TAXES

If ye be willing and obedient, ye shall
eat the good of the land.

—ISAIAH 1:19

Yea, the LORD shall give that which is good;
and our land shall yield her increase.

—PSALM 85:12

Have you ever heard the phrase, "The only things certain in life are death and taxes"? It is true. If you work, you are going to pay taxes, and there is no way around it. People try to avoid giving Uncle Sam what they owe him, but the government will *always* get what belongs to it. For this reason, it is important to recognize the importance of paying your taxes in a timely manner and filing your tax returns properly. Whether you enlist the help of a tax professional or do your taxes yourself, it is your responsibility to pay taxes on any income you earn over the course of the year.

The IRS is a bureau of the Department of the Treasury and is responsible for making sure that all American citizens meet their tax responsibilities. They are also responsible for enforcing the law as it relates to citizens paying their taxes. The mission of the IRS can be summed up in these three points:

- In the United States, Congress passes tax laws and requires taxpayers to comply.
- The taxpayer's role is to understand and meet his or her tax obligations.
- The IRS's role is to help the large majority of compliant taxpayers with tax law, while ensuring that the minority who are unwilling to comply pay their fair share.

As law-abiding citizens, we are required to pay taxes if we live and work in this country. There are people who feel they should not have to pay taxes, for one reason or another, but we are required to abide by these laws. Even Jesus paid His taxes! As Christians we should always be eager to obey the laws of the land because in doing that we are submitting to the civil authorities that God has instituted. Instead of looking for loopholes and ways to avoid doing what we are required to do, we should be willing to pay what we owe.

As law-abiding citizens, we are required to pay taxes if we live and work in this country.

With that being said, it is important that we file our tax returns properly to ensure that we pay the right amount to the IRS and also receive tax breaks if they apply to us. There are different ways to file your taxes. For example, you can pay a tax professional to prepare your taxes for you, or you can do them yourself. Numerous online tax preparation Web sites allow you to file your taxes yourself. These programs make it easy for you to complete the filing process by inputting all the information into forms online that calculate how much you owe or how much of a refund you will receive. The beauty of it is that the program does the work for you. You just have to make sure that you enter all the information accurately. Fortunately, these online tax prep programs allow you to review your return before submitting it, as well as alert you to any errors or missing information prior to filing.

What Basic Forms to Use

Form 1040EZ is one of the simplest forms to use when filing your taxes. You qualify to use this form if:

- Your taxable income is under $100,000.

- Your interest income is under $1,500.

- You have income only from wages, interest, unemployment compensation, and Alaska Permanent Fund dividends.

- You and your spouse are under sixty-five years old.

- Your filing status is single or married filing jointly.

- You do not have any adjustments to income.

- You are claiming only the standard deductions.

- You may claim the Earned Income Credit.

- You are not claiming any other tax credits.

Most taxpayers qualify to use Form 1040A, often called the "short form." This form allows you to claim the most common adjustments to income and is available for all ages and filing statuses. You can use this form if:

- Your taxable income is under $100,000.

- You have income from wages, interest, dividends, capital gain distributions, IRA or pension distributions, unemployment compensation, or Social Security benefits.

- You can claim the following adjustments to income: penalty for early withdrawal of savings,

IRA contributions, student loan interest, and jury duty pay given to your employer.

- You can claim the following tax credits: child and dependent care credit, credit for the elderly and disabled, education credits, retirement savings contributions credit, child tax credit, and earned income credit.

You cannot use Form 1040A if you want to itemize your deductions. Most taxpayers qualify to use Form 1040A; however, there may be income and deductions found on the longer Form 1040 that would make it a better option. Be sure to look over Form 1040 as well to determine if you should use it.

Form 1040 is also known as "the long form" and can be used by *any* taxpayer. It takes longer to fill out but it covers any tax situation. This is a required form if:

- You have income of $100,000 or more.

- You are itemizing your deductions (such as mortgage interest or charity).

- You have income from a rental, business, farm, S-corporation, partnership, or trust.

- You have foreign wages, paid foreign taxes, or are claiming tax treaty benefits.

- You sold stocks, bonds, mutual funds, or property.

- You are claiming adjustments to income for educator expenses, tuition and fees, moving expenses, or health savings accounts.

Form 1040 is the form to use if you have any questions or concerns about what form is the best option for you.

Filing Basics

To file your taxes, you will need your W-2 form from your employer. This form documents your yearly wages as well as how much tax was withheld from your paycheck. It will also have other information on it such as your employer identification number and your Social Security number. Your employer must provide you with this form prior to the deadline set by the IRS.

If you have made any other income over the year, you may need to obtain additional forms to report this income. For example, if you did independent contract work for a company or are self-employed, you will need to report income from Form 1099-MISC. Just as you receive a W-2 from your employer, the company for whom you did contract work will provide you with this form.

If you are doing your taxes via an online tax preparation program such as TurboTax or TaxACT, all you need to do is create an account and follow the instructions and prompts. You will need to make sure that you have all the necessary forms, such as your W-2 Forms, a 1099 if applicable, and any other paperwork that is required. If you will be reporting your charitable giving to a non-profit organization, make sure you have your giving statements on hand so that your totals are accurate. If you are in business for yourself, you will be prompted to enter in anything that was purchased for business purposes, including gas for traveling to and from a client and other expenses. Be sure to keep all your receipts for these purposes if you are an independent business owner. All of these things are tax write-offs that can lower your tax balance and even put money back in your pocket. The same is true for charitable donations, which will contribute to reducing your tax balance and give you a bigger refund.

*Be sure to keep all your receipts for these purposes if
you are an independent business owner.*

Being a homeowner is a huge benefit come tax season because
there are significant tax write-offs you can take advantage of.
Consider the following:

- Mortgage Fee Deductions

When you purchase a home or refinance your home, there are
fees involved. Some are tax-deductible. You can typically write off
mortgage fees such as prepaid interest, origination fees, and loan
discount fees.

- Property Taxes

You can deduct your property taxes from your federal tax
returns. This is an annual deduction you can take each year you
live in the home.

- Mortgage Interest

Generally, you can also write off the entire interest portion of
your home loan payment on your taxes as well. A typical fifteen-
to thirty-year fixed-rate mortgage is mostly interest for about the
first half of the mortgage term anyway, so you are truly maximiz-
ing your tax deduction during those years.

- Private Mortgage Insurance

When a lender finances more than 80 percent of the purchase
price of a home, it typically requires private mortgage insurance,
also known as PMI. This usually remains part of your home
loan payment until you pay down the mortgage so that it is only

80 percent of the value of the home. While PMI is not typically expensive, it is also a payment that is tax deductible.

- Selling Costs

When you sell your home, you also have the right to deduct some of the costs. Some of the selling costs you can typically deduct include real estate agent commissions, title insurance, legal fees, advertising, administrative costs, inspection fees, and repair and redecorating costs up to ninety days before the sale of the property.

When you really look at the tax benefits of being a homeowner, it becomes clear why it should be a priority. As a renter, not only are you putting money in someone else's pocket and not reaping any benefit from it, but you are locked out of the tax write-offs that can help to lower your tax bill and possibly bring a refund into your hands. If you are not a homeowner, now is the time to start looking into making the investment.

There are other tax write-offs you should consider in addition to homeownership. Significant interest accrued on student loans may qualify as a write-off, as well as health insurance premiums that you pay (added to medical expenses, and they have to exceed 7.5 percent of your adjusted gross income before taxes), and retirement savings tax credits. There are other credits you may qualify for, so be sure to consult with a tax professional. Many times more write-offs are available to people, but they never benefit from them because they just don't know. The official Web site of the IRS is a great resource for obtaining this information.

If you complete your taxes and find that you owe the IRS money you don't have at the time, you can set up a payment plan. Contact www.irs.gov for more information on how to set up a payment plan. The key is not to neglect paying your taxes. God will get involved with your situation when you do your part. Also, be sure to have enough taxes taken out of your paycheck during the year so that you do not owe money come tax season.

The key is not to neglect paying your taxes.

Paying taxes may seem like a hassle, but remember, taxes are what keep our country going. The amenities we enjoy as citizens in this country are funded by tax dollars. Rather than complaining about paying taxes, commit to honoring the laws of the land, which essentially means submitting to those in authority who have set up institutions such as the IRS to make sure that we pay our taxes. As we maintain a good attitude toward civil authorities and the laws that have been implemented for our good, we honor God and position ourselves for favor and blessings in our finances and in every other area of our lives.

GLOSSARY OF TERMS

- **Risk Tolerance**—The degree of uncertainty that an investor can handle in regard to negative change in the value of his or her portfolio.

- **Stocks**—The original capital paid into or invested in a business by its founders. It serves as a <u>security</u> for the <u>creditors</u> of a business since it cannot be withdrawn to the detriment of the creditors.

- **Bonds**—Certificates that represent money a government or corporation has borrowed from other entities.

- **Certificate of Deposit (CD)**—A short- to medium-term, FDIC-insured investment available at banks and savings and loan institutions.

- **Mutual Funds**—A type of professionally managed <u>collective investment vehicle</u> that pools money from many investors to purchase <u>securities</u>. Mutual funds are typically regulated and available to the general public.

- **IRA**—Also known as an Individual Retirement Account, this is a savings account with big tax breaks, making it an ideal way to save cash for your retirement.

- **Real estate**—Property consisting of land and the buildings on it, along with its natural resources such as crops, minerals, or water; immovable property of this nature; an interest vested in this; buildings or housing in general.

- **Trust**—A written agreement between two parties. The trustor, or grantor, establishes the trust, and the bank, person, or persons who manage it, is the trustee or trustees. The trust agreement details how the trust operates during the grantor's life and what happens to the assets following his or her death.

- **Power of Attorney**—A written authorization to represent or act on another's behalf in private affairs, business, or some other legal matter. The person authorizing the other to act is the *principal, grantor,* or *donor* (of the power), and the one authorized to act is the *agent, donee,* or *attorney.*

- **Will**—A legal declaration by which a person, the testator, names one or more persons to manage his estate and provides for the transfer of his property at death.

- **Checking Account**—A transactional deposit account held at a financial institution that allows for withdrawals and deposits.

- **Savings Account**—A deposit account held at a bank or other financial institution that provides principal security and a modest interest rate.

- **Life Insurance**—Insurance that pays out a sum of money either on the death of the insured person or after a set period.

- **IRS**—Internal Revenue Service.

STUDY CENTER

Recommended Resources

Financial Web sites

www.ironmanfinancial.com

www.msmoney.com

www.moneymanagement.org

www.mint.com

www.suzeorman.com

www.ml.com

www.schwab.com

www.fidelity.com

www.scottrade.com

www.sharebuilder.com

www.crediteducation.org

www.consumercredit.com

www.experian.com

www.equifax.com

www.transunion.com

www.ingdirect.com

www.irs.gov

www.taxactonline.com

www.turbotax.com

Books

The Automatic Millionaire by David Bach

The Finish Rich book series by David Bach

God's Plan for Your Money by Derek Prince

Becoming a Millionaire God's Way by Dr. C. Thomas Anderson

Master Your Money by Ron Blue

Personal Finances by Larry Burkett

Understanding the Spirituality of True Stewardship by Christopher N. Sealey

The Intelligent Investor by Benjamin Graham

The Total Money Makeover: A Proven Plan for Financial Fitness by Dave Ramsey

Financial Peace Revisited by Dave Ramsey

The Real Book of Real Estate: Real Experts. Real Stories. Real Life by Robert T. Kiyosaki

The Money Class: How to Stand in Your Truth and Create the Future You Deserve by Suze Orman

The Financial Peace Planner: A Step-by-Step Guide to Restoring Your Family's Financial Health by Dave Ramsey

Make Your Own Living Trust by Dennis Clifford

The Behavior Gap: Simple Ways to Stop Doing Dumb Things with Money by Carl Richards

The Investment Answer by Daniel C. Goldie and Gordan S. Murray

The Intelligent Asset Allocator: How to Build Your Portfolio to Maximize Returns and Minimize Risk by William Bernstein

The Budget Kit: The Common Cents Money Management Workbook by Judy Lawrence

The Wall Street Journal Complete Money and Investing Guidebook by Dave Kansas